FOREIGN ECONOMIC POLICY OF THE UNITED STATES

Edited by
STUART BRUCHEY
Columbia University

A GARLAND SERIES

FOREIGN ECONOMIC POLICY OF THE UNITED STATES

Financial Diplomacy:
The United States and Mexico
1919–1933

STEPHEN D. BODAYLA

GARLAND PUBLISHING, INC.
NEW YORK & LONDON • 1987

Copyright © 1987 Stephen D. Bodayla
All rights reserved

For a complete list of the titles in this series,
see the final pages of this volume.

Library of Congress Cataloging-in-Publication Data

Bodayla, Stephen D.
  Financial diplomacy.

  (Foreign economic policy of the United States)
  Thesis (Ph.D.)--New York University, 1975.
  Bibliography: p.
  1. United States--Foreign economic relations--Mexico.
2. Mexico--Foreign economic relations--United States.
3. United States--Foreign relations--20th century.
4. Mexico--Foreign relations--1910-1946. I. Title.
II. Series.
HF1456.5.M6B63 1987   337.73072   87-23790
ISBN 0-8240-8074-2

All volumes in this series are printed on acid-free,
250-year-life paper.

Printed in the United States of America

TABLE OF CONTENTS

INTRODUCTION...................................... ix

CHAPTER   PAGE

I. EARLY CRISES OF THE MEXICAN REPUBLIC.......... 1
    Financial plight of the early republic...... 2
    French intervention......................... 3
    Juárez years................................ 6
    Díaz revolution............................. 9
    Díaz fiscal policy.......................... 11
    Madero revolution........................... 25
    American intervention....................... 32
    Constitution of 1917........................ 34

II. INTERNATIONAL COMMITTEE OF BANKERS ON MEXICO.. 36
    Friction between United States and Carranza. 36
    Formation of the International Committee.... 39
    Intervention crisis of 1919................. 44
    Overthrow of Carranza....................... 49
    Hughes policy towards Mexico................ 55
    Lamont-de la Huerta agreement............... 61
    Bucareli agreement.......................... 65
    De la Huerta revolt......................... 66
    Failure of the Lamont-de la Huerta agreement 68

CHAPTER	PAGE
III. AMBASSADOR JAMES ROCKWELL SHEFFIELD	70
Appointment of Sheffield	71
Secretary of State Frank B. Kellogg	73
Sheffield's philosophy	76
Lamont-Pani agreement	80
Petroleum controversy	81
Influence of Robert E. Olds on State Department policy toward Mexico	84
Sheffield becomes an obstacle to policy execution	87
Church-state conflict	95
Nicaragua intervention	96
Resignation of Sheffield	104
IV. AMBASSADOR DWIGHT W. MORROW	105
Morrow's background and experience	106
Morrow's appointment as ambassador	110
Changing State Department policy	113
Resolution of oil controversy	122
Sterrett-Davis report	135
Obregón's assassination	137
V. DISAGREEMENT BETWEEN MORROW AND LAMONT	143
McBride's recommendations on Mexican debt question	145
Morrow's influence on Mexican leaders	148

CHAPTER PAGE

    Morrow and Mexican insolvency................151
    Morrow opposes new agreement.................157
    State Department supports Morrow.............158
    Impact of Escobar revolution.................161
    Clark "Memorandum on Monroe Doctrine".......164
    Resolution of Church-State conflict..........168
    Policy of Secretary of State Henry L. Stimson..171
    Moderation of land reform program............174

VI. MORROW VERSUS LAMONT............................177
    Impact of Morrow's absence from Mexico......177
    Conflict between Lamont and Morrow over proposed agreement........................182
    Lamont-Montes de Oca agreement..............185
    Opposition of State Department to agreement.186
    Influence of Morrow on delay of ratification....................................190
    Morrow resigns ambassadorship...............191
    Hoover-Stimson policy toward Latin America..192
    Appointment of J. Reuben Clark Jr. as ambassador................................195
    Failure of Lamont-Montes de Oca agreement...196
    Impact of Depression on Mexico..............198

CHAPTER   PAGL

    Appointment of Ambassador Josephus Daniels..203

    Collapse of negotiations between Mexico

        and International Committee of Bankers....204

CONCLUSION...206

BIBLIOGRAPHY...210

INTRODUCTION

The iron hand of Porfirio Díaz brought almost four decades of stability to Mexico. Relations with the United States were cordial; foreign investments were secure. The Madero revolution of 1911 inaugurated an era of instability which jeopardized Mexican-American relations and aroused the anxieties of American and European investors.

The purpose of this study is to analyze and evaluate the attempts of the Department of State and the International Committee of Bankers on Mexico, in the years 1919-1924, to cooperate in normalizing Mexican-American relations, stabilizing the country's economy and protecting foreign investments. The study also tries to explain the reasons for the eventual failure of the cooperative effort and the emergence of an embryonic "good neighbor" policy. Attempts are made to answer several fundamental questions. What was the nature of the friction between the United States and Mexico? Why did the State Department work with private financial interests? What were the goals of the bankers? To what extent was the cooperation successful? What were the obstacles encountered? Why did the cooperation cease? Why, how and when did the "good neighbor" policy begin?

This monograph relies heavily on the papers of the chief diplomatic "actors", government documents (both published and unpublished) and the memoirs and reminiscences of those involved in the formulation and execution of foreign policy on both sides of the border. Specialized studies of specific aspects of Mexican-American relations and financial diplomacy between 1919 and 1933 also have been consulted. The bibliography is composed solely of those materials cited in the footnotes, although scores of other works were examined.

CHAPTER I

EARLY CRISES OF THE MEXICAN REPUBLIC

The first half-century after Mexico won its independence was characterized by almost constant domestic strife, frequently humiliating international relations and a disconcerting tendency toward fiscal irresponsibility. It was not until Porfirio Díaz seized the presidency from Sebastian Lerdo de Tejada in 1876 that Mexico was to enjoy a degree of domestic tranquility which would win it the tolerance granted by powerful nations to their weaker but stable brethren.

Díaz was to dominate Mexico from the time of his <u>coup d'état</u> until the aged dictator suddenly resigned the presidency on May 25, 1911, and fled into exile in Europe. Blessed with thirty-five consecutive years of rule (including one term for a stand-in), Díaz was able gradually to solidify his autocratic hold until he appeared unchallengable. With the unwavering support of the military, large landholders and the entrepreneurial class, Díaz succeeded in establishing Mexico's first enduring government since independence. To achieve this happy condition it was necessary that Díaz isolate Mexico from the kinds of political and social change that were occurring elsewhere in a rapidly industrializing world.

It was under Díaz too that Mexico's foreign relations and financial condition improved. The political chaos that had typified the pre-Díaz years brought Mexico into frequent and sometimes costly disagreements with the United States and several European nations. To the United States Mexico lost the vast, rich northern territory of Texas and the area west to the Pacific. This was a national humiliation not easily forgotten. Mexico's fiscal debility too brought it into embarrassing international predicaments.

In 1824 and 1825 Mexico had floated on the London market two sterling loans totalling ₤6.4 million designed to assist the government in maintaining its newly-won independence. Initially the interest on these issues was met out of funds which the underwriting bankers had retained specifically for that purpose. In 1827, when these funds were exhausted, Mexico defaulted without paying any interest from current revenues.[1]

The Mexican-American War and almost six decades of domestic turmoil had made it impossible for Mexico to honor its debts despite several short-lived, negotiated settlements. Chief among these were agreements concluded by diplomatic conventions in 1851 with Britain and Spain.[2] Po-

---

[1] William H. Wynne, *State Insolvency and Foreign Bondholders* (New Haven, 1951), 5-13.

[2] For details of these convention agreements see *ibid.*, 14-19, and Edgar Turlington, *Mexico and Her Foreign Creditors* (New York, 1930), 100-104.

litical chaos continued to play havoc with orderly administration and severely retarded economic growth.

In 1861 the government of Benito Juárez, fighting a civil war, was unable to meet the claims lodged by England, France and Spain on behalf of their nationals. As a result of Mexico's dire financial plight, Juárez had declared a two-year moratorium on all external national debts.[3] A Swiss banker (now a French citizen) had contracted with an earlier Mexican government to loan 15 million pesos at six percent interest. The actual rate of return has been estimated as high as 90 percent as a result of fraudulent manipulations by the banker and corrupt Mexican officials. Although less than ten percent of the promised loan was actually delivered, he pressured the French government to challenge the Juárez moratorium.[4] The anti-Juárez elements intimated to the government of Napoleon III that they would honor the claims of European nationals in exchange for French support against Juárez.[5] Since the United States was occupied with its own

---

[3] In 1861 the external debt, together with more than nine years' interest arrears, was estimated at about 74 million pesos. "Memorandum on the Public Debt of Mexico," dated May 20, 1928, Dwight W. Morrow Papers, Amherst College Library, Amherst, Massachusetts. (Hereafter cited as Morrow Papers.)

[4] The fraudulent nature of this loan by J.B. Jecker and Company is clearly described in Turlington, Mexico and Her Foreign Creditors, 116-117.

[5] One of the best studies in English of the Juárez years is Walter V. Scholes, Mexican Politics during the Juárez Regime, 1855-1872 (Columbia, Mo., 1957).

destructive Civil War, it was not in a position to prevent a European violation of the Monroe Doctrine. Uninhibited by American opposition, France, Britain and Spain dispatched warships to Veracruz.

While overtly Napoleon voiced interest in protecting the property of French citizens, in reality he was pursuing significantly greater stakes. Aware that Mexico could not possibly meet its obligations, Napoleon pressed still larger claims to justify the sending of troops to Mexico, apparently as a preliminary step to bringing that nation under his ambitious wing. When Britain and Spain became suspicious of Napoleon's imperialistic goals, they recalled their forces on April 28, 1862.[6]

With the aid of Mexican anti-Juárez conservatives, the French expeditionary force succeeded in crushing the liberal Republican resistance and driving the Juárez regime out of Mexico City. Mexican monarchists joined with Napoleon in selecting the Austrian Maximilian as emperor of Mexico. All the major world powers except the United States soon recognized Maximilian's government. Napoleon agreed that French troops would remain in Mexico until 1867 and Maximilian promised that all foreign claims would be paid and the cost

---

[6]Howard F. Cline, The United States and Mexico (rev. ed., Cambridge, 1967), 47-48.

of French intervention would be reimbursed by Mexico. Additionally, in 1864 Mexico obtained a six percent loan for L12,365,000 with L8 million offered on the London and Paris markets and the balance taken up by the French government. It was hoped that the bond offering would enable Mexico to reorganize its chaotic national finances.[7]

Maximilian's commitments increased Mexico's national debt threefold. The new loan was inadequate to meet Mexico's obligations; the large discount rate and the deduction of interest arrears on the earlier debt reduced the proceeds available by two-thirds. Worse yet, 99 percent of the revenues from customs duties had been assigned for the payment of interest on the new loans, the cost of intervention, and the earlier debts owed to Britain and Spain.[8]

While French troops remained in Mexico the moderately liberal Maximilian was able to hold in check the dissidents. But with the American Civil War successfully ended, Secretary of State William Seward reminded Paris of the Monroe Doctrine and this, combined with Prussia's victory over Austria (which aroused Napoleon's anxieties as to Bismarck's intentions), forced the French to withdraw their troops from Mexico early in 1867. Soon thereafter, on June 20, 1867,

---

[7] Wynne, State Insolvency, 27-28.

[8] Turlington, Mexico and Her Foreign Creditors, 153-158.

the Republican forces of Juárez captured Mexico City and executed Maximilian.[9]

Juárez immediately called for a new election. His term had expired during the reign of Maximilian. With no organized conservative opposition, Juárez handily defeated the moderate liberal General Porfirio Díaz.

In the wake of his victory Juárez attempted to reduce government spending and lessen the likelihood of future military coups by reducing the army by some 60,000 men. In so doing he antagonized the veterans whom he released without pensions and were easily attracted to Díaz' opposition group.

Juárez aroused anxieties internationally when he repudiated the loans contracted by Maximilian and all custom duty assignments made by him. Circumstances in Europe resulting from Bismarck's machinations ruled out the possibility that France and Britain would again resort to the use of force to collect debts owed to their nationals. France, in fact, reimbursed French investors for approximately 50 percent of their investment in Maximilian's bonds.[10]

Yet it was the repudiation of the pre-intervention assignments of customs duties that shocked the European powers the most. Juárez justified this action on the grounds that

---

[9] Cline, The United States and Mexico, 48-49.

[10] Turlington, Mexico and Her Foreign Creditors, 172-173.

Britain and Spain had joined with France in the early intervention which had violated Mexican sovereignty and afterward had recognized Maximilian's government and had even entered into new accords with his government in regard to the debt. These actions, Juárez maintained, abrogated all previous agreements between these nations and the republican government. Juárez was quick to state however, that the Mexican government did not "deny the obligation of the national treasury to pay the legitimate and recognized titles .... All that it denies is...that the terms of payment stipulated in a no longer existing arrangement should subsist."[11]

In 1868 Juárez authorized a claims convention with the United States to settle all outstanding claims between the two nations. The commission found that Mexico owed the United States approximately 2,874,000 pesos net. This sum was subsequently paid in cash installments.[12] The action demonstrated Juárez' firm determination to honor debts and claims properly incurred.

The Juárez government adopted a program by which it would make available not less than 50,000 pesos each month

---

[11] Edward L. Plumb to William H. Seward, February 12, 1868. United States. Department of State. Papers Relating to the Foreign Relations of the United States...1868 (2 vols., Washington, D.C., 1868), II, 419. (Hereafter cited as FRUS.)

[12] "Memorandum on the Public Debt of Mexico," May 20, 1928, Morrow Papers.

for the purchase at "auction" of the largest quantity tendered of bonds of the British and Spanish convention. This method proved to be quite successful, with approximately 1.1 million pesos in bonds acquired for only 204,995 pesos cash by May 1868.[13] At this rate, several years would be required to redeem the entire debt. But numerous groups were working to render the completion of the project unsuccessful.

Juárez' term expired in 1871 and in the new election he was opposed by vice-president Lerdo de Tejada and General Díaz. Although attracting the most votes, Juárez fell short of a majority, but he was designated president by the Chamber of Deputies. Díaz supporters claimed that the election was rigged and called for a new constitution which would, among other things, prohibit a president from succeeding himself. In the midst of the controversy Juárez died and was succeeded by vice-president Lerdo de Tejada, who became provisional president in July 1872. A special election returned him to the executive office, but it seemed to antagonize Díaz still further.

During the Lerdo de Tejada presidency numerous abortive attempts were made at a final settlement of Mexico's

---

[13]Turlington, Mexico and Her Foreign Creditors, 176-177; Second Annual Report of the Council of the Corporation of Foreign Bondholders (London, 1874), 44-45.

foreign debts. Meanwhile, two offerings of bonds of the Mexican Railway Company totalling ₤1,440,000 were made on the London market in 1871 and 1874. These bonds were secured by an assignment of Mexico's customs revenues, although these revenues already had been assigned as security against the earlier London loan. Disturbed by these actions, the London-based Committee of Mexican Bondholders succeeded in obtaining a commitment from the European bourses enabling it to inform the Mexican government that it could no longer raise capital through offerings on the European money markets.[14]

When Lerdo declared himself to be the winner in an apparently fraudulent presidential election in 1876, Díaz headed a popular rebellion that overthrew Lerdo and sent him into exile. Earlier Díaz had declared that any agreement Lerdo concluded with the English bondholders would be null and void. In order to raise new revenues he enacted a tax on profits derived from all classes of property. In an effort to win the recognition of the United States, Díaz decreed that a portion of the revenues from this tax would be applied to debt due the United States as fixed by the claims commission under the convention of July 4, 1868.[15]

---

[14]Wynne, State Insolvency, 34-36.

[15]Turlington, Mexico and Her Foreign Creditors, 187-190. For discussion of the decisions of this commission, which terminated its existence in 1876, see Frederick S. Dunn, The Diplomatic Protection of Americans in Mexico (New York, 1933), ch. IV.

In response to this gesture, the State Department, on January 19, 1877, authorized American Minister John W. Foster to recognize the Díaz government.[16]

Díaz was reaffirmed as president by the electorate early in 1877 and assumed office constitutionally on April 2, 1877. By March 1878 he enjoyed the recognition of Germany, Spain and the United States. Yet all was not well in Mexico. The nation was suffering economic stagnation. Employees of all the departments of government except the legislative had salaries in arrears. Public works projects were held up because of a lack of funds. Foreign trade had declined drastically while smuggling had increased. Rumors of new taxes raised anxieties among the propertied and business elements. These conditions compelled Foster to report to the State Department that there was "very little hope of an early redemption or rather commencement of payment of interest" on bonds held by Americans; and he also expressed fears that Mexico's financial embarrassment would again lead to revolution.[17] Foster proved to be overly pessimistic.

Díaz had dealt swiftly and brutally with those who opposed him. All rebels were summarily executed. He avoided

---

[16] William M. Evarts to John W. Foster, January 19, 1877. FRUS 1877, 385-395.

[17] Foster to Evarts, October 25, 1878. FRUS 1878, 660-661.

the constitutional stipulation that a president could not succeed himself by causing General Manuel González to be elected in November 1880, with Díaz remaining the power behind the throne.

In 1884 Díaz once again gained direct control of the government through his reelection to the presidency. To perpetuate his power, he brought about still another constitutional reform in 1887 which allowed him to seek reelection. Three years later the Mexican Congress felt obliged to annul the article forbidding reelection, thus allowing Díaz to be returned to office each election through 1910.

With the security provided by these constitutional maneuvers, Díaz aggressively tackled the debt problem. Desirous of attracting new foreign capital to Mexico, Díaz realized that it was imperative that the default on the foreign debt be settled and that the nation's deficit budget be returned to the black through drastic reductions in government spending and consolidation of internal debt.[18]

Early in his second term Díaz appointed a commission to analyze Mexico's financial condition and submit comprehensive recommendations for its rectification. On June 22, 1885, he issued three presidential decrees inspired by the commissions recommendations. One decree, aimed at reducing the

---

[18] For a recent analysis of Mexico's foreign debts, see: Jan Bazant, La deuda exterior de México (Mexico City, 1968).

government payroll, provided for temporary reduction in the salaries of all civil and military employees earning in excess of 500 pesos. A second decree required the consolidation of the floating debt contracted between July 1, 1882, and June 30, 1885, into a new six percent Treasury bond issue of 25 million pesos maturing in 1910. The final decree dealt with the unconsolidated debts incurred before July 1, 1882, the London debt and the abrogated English and Spanish convention debts. Díaz called for the tendering of these issues in exchange for new unsecured three percent bonds. This issue would initially pay only one percent interest in 1886 but would increase by ½ percent each year until it reached the full three percent in 1890. All debts were to be exchanged at par with no consideration for interest arrears, which were to be negotiated with the creditors.[19]

Díaz moved quickly to secure the acquiesence of all creditors to the aforementioned exchanges. On June 23, 1886, an agreement was reached with the London Bondholders Committee by which this group accepted the terms for the conversion of the principal of the London debt and agreed that interest arrears on that debt would be exchanged for new three

---

[19]Wynne, State Insolvency, 39-40; Turlington, Mexico and Her Foreign Creditors, 205-207.

percent bonds.[20]

Shortly thereafter, on December 30, 1886, an accord was reached in regard to the English convention debt by which the outstanding bonds with interest arrears would also be exchanged for the three percent bonds.[21] The Spanish convention debts were resolved in a similar manner on May 1, 1890.[22]

The Mexican negotiators had insisted that each accord include a provision granting the government the right to purchase the new bonds at market value or to call them at 40 percent of their face value. This was to prove a very perspicacious approach to Mexico's financial rehabilitation. The London debt, which with interest arrears had totalled approximately £22 million, was converted into £14 million in three percent bonds, redeemable within two years for approximately £5.5 million in cash. The English convention debt was redeemed for only £350,000. The Spanish convention debt experienced a similar discount.[23]

---

[20] The interest arrears were represented by bonds issued by Maximilian in 1864 in lieu of interest payments. Together with their coupons, these bonds were to be exchanged for new 3 percent bonds at the rate of £50 for each £100 old, with coupons attached and 15 percent for unpaid coupons of 1866 through 1886. Wynne, State Insolvency, 40.

[21] The exchange rate was to be £150 new bonds for each 500 pesos old with coupons attached.

[22] Bonds with coupons were to be exchanged for 3 percent bonds at 145 percent of principal amount of the old bonds.

[23] Turlington, Mexico and Her Foreign Creditors, 205-211.

The benefits of this financial reorganization scheme for Mexico were myriad. Loans in default since 1827 were redeemed for cash in an amount about equal to the original figure, with almost sixty years of interest arrears virtually wiped out. Still more astounding, the cunning Díaz succeeded in redeeming at 40 percent of face amount the new three percent bonds, using for the purpose a portion of the proceeds of a new foreign loan obtained in 1888. He accomplished this through a privilege allowed Mexico in the agreements with the holders of the London and convention bonds.[24]

The 1888 loan was possible because Díaz had shrewdly taken advantage of the good-will resulting from his aggressive moves toward settlement of the long-standing foreign debt. Floated in Europe, this new loan was designed to relieve Mexico's serious domestic financial problems. In 1888 Mexican bonds in the amount of ₤10.5 million were offered in Europe by German and English bankers; the issue was eagerly oversubscribed. Approximately two-thirds of the proceeds were used to redeem the three percent consolidated bonds at 40 percent of face amount.[25]

The decade of the 1890's dawned on a positive note. Díaz had effectively restored Mexico's credit rating on the

---

[24] Wynne, State Insolvency, 45-46.

[25] Ibid., 47-48.

world's money markets. New infusions of foreign capital enabled Mexico to begin an ambitious public works program, including the construction of canals, railway lines and roads, the deepening of harbors, the extension of drainage systems, construction of telephone and telegraph lines and improvement of water supplies. Díaz won new respect internationally for having brought order to what was commonly considered to be a hopeless situation.

The foreign bondholders generally were quite pleased with the turnaround Mexico was exhibiting under Díaz. The foreign debt had been honored reasonably well, considering Mexico's real capabilities at the time. Díaz promised a government of peace and order and seemed well on his way toward achieving both. The only disconcerting note was the large amounts of railroad subsidies being granted annually. By 1889, 23 percent of the customs revenues had been assigned for payment of these subsidies.[26]

Díaz had resorted to subsidies because private investors were unwilling to risk capital in railroad ventures across a country yet undeveloped and sparsely populated. Díaz considered railroads essential to the development of Mexico, and to get them built he granted substantial subsidies, sometimes at the expense of other obligations. He

---

[26]Turlington, Mexico and Her Foreign Creditors, 216.

negotiated large loans in Europe to raise funds for this ambitious railroad construction program at a time when Mexico still owed significant sums from earlier loans.[27]

Díaz apparently believed that the numerous problems that Mexico experienced since winning its independence had their genesis not in political instability or in social unrest but in the state's chronically pitiful economic condition. From this perspective it is not difficult to understand his disregard for individual liberties and democracy. These he saw as luxuries and they must wait. Democracy, social equality, freedom would come with the cessation of civil wars and foreign interventions, which would follow when Mexico achieved solvency.

This is not to say that Díaz was totally ruthless in his administration of government in order to achieve his ends. In actuality Díaz took steps to reconcile the divergent interests and factions in order that progress might be made more thoroughly and more efficiently. Still it must be conceded that opposition was hardly tolerated, elections

---

[27]Generally these subsidies were direct incentives to spur rail line construction and were paid per mile of rail laid. Only the Mexican Railway Company received a fixed sum annually. Wynne, State Insolvency, 49-51; Fred W. Powell, The Railways of Mexico (Boston, 1921), 169-172.

were anything but democratic and political oppression was not uncommon.[28]

Díaz met frequent obstacles in his quest to restore Mexico to fiscal responsibility. A succession of bad harvests in 1890-1892 brought Mexico to the brink of famine. The government found it necessary to purchase large quantities of maize from the United States. Meanwhile, a continuing decline in silver prices resulted in a *de facto* increase in the external debt service. These combined to jeopardize the debt settlements of the 1880's, which some officials in the administration were prepared to allow to go into default. Only the placement, in 1893, of some Ł2.5 million in six percent secured bonds in London avoided an immediate default.[29]

Simultaneous with this loan the Mexican Congress authorized Díaz to readjust the internal debt which, despite the 1885 consolidation effort, had remained in unsatisfactory condition. A portion of the outstanding credits and claims had not yet been exchanged for the three percent bonds. Additionally, new floating indebtedness contracted after June 1885 remained unsettled. By a decree issued in

---

[28]Cline, The United States and Mexico, 51-54; See also Wilfred H. Callcott, Liberalism in Mexico, 1857-1929 (Palo Alto, 1931), which places Díaz in a broader political perspective.

[29]This loan was one of desperation as evidenced by the offering price of 63. It was secured on 12 percent of the customs duties. Wynne, State Insolvency, 51-52.

September 1894 all of the above outstanding debts and the various issues of bonds allotted as railway subsidies were to be converted "at or above par" into new five percent bonds. These new bonds were tax exempt and redeemable at par.[30]

Diaz' approach to Mexico's problems was greatly influenced by the positivist philosophy embraced by the new capitalists of the right who considered order the fundamental ingredient of progress. Those who espoused this position maintained that the state was the guardian of the material order in which the rights of individuals must be limited by the rights of others. Within this framework, wealth was, in the hands of the rich, an instrument used for the common good and for progress. All that the wealthy needed to do was use their riches to stimulate more material wealth in the national economy.[31]

It was the científicos, an elite inner circle within the Union Liberal Party formed in 1892, who first attempted to transform this philosophy into politics. With Diaz at the helm the científicos were able to bring about greater commercial and economic opportunities for the monied class.

---

[30] Ibid., 52-54.

[31] For a fuller discussion of the philosophy of the científicos see Leopoldo Zea, El positivismo en Mexico (Mexico City, 1953), 173-180.

Chief exponent of the científicos philosophy was José Yves Limantour, who had become Mexico's Minister of Finance in 1893. With the support and friendship of Díaz, Limantour was able to pursue aggressively programs aimed at further strengthening Mexico's economy. The internal tax structure was overhauled, revenue collections were streamlined and new capital was courted actively.[32] As a reflection of his remarkable success, the period 1895 to 1899 showed annual cash surpluses from current government operations.[33]

Foreign investors and speculators were enticed by Mexico's abundant, undeveloped natural resources and the generous concessions and subsidies offered by the Díaz regime. When combined with the domestic stability and efficient administration Díaz had demonstrated, these opportunities convinced financiers in the United States, Britain and Germany to propose new loans at significantly improved terms over those of 1888, 1889 and 1893.

In 1899 and 1904, Limantour concluded on behalf of his government new agreements with terms clearly advantageous to Mexico. By virtue of the 1899 accord German, English and American investment bankers, led by J.P. Morgan & Company and S. Bleichroeder of Berlin, contracted to consolidate

---

[32]Cline, The United States and Mexico, 54-55.

[33]"Memorandum on the Public Debt of Mexico," dated May 20, 1928, Morrow Papers.

the entire foreign debt through the issuance of ₤22.7 million in new five percent bonds. These would be offered in exchange for old bonds at par with cash bonuses of from 1 to 2 percent, depending on the issue tendered. Holders of approximately 75 percent of the outstanding foreign debt exchanged their securities for the new issue. The balance was redeemed for cash raised through the sale of ₤5 million of the bonds on the New York and Amsterdam money markets. The conversion saved Mexico approximately ₤117,000 annually in interest payments.[34]

The 1904 loan, also handled by a syndicate of American and European banking houses, offered four percent gold bonds for $40 million, $25 million of which were placed privately, with the balance sold on major money markets. This offering reflected a changing Mexican policy arising out of the prolonged decline in the price of silver which had caused an almost constant fluctuation in exchange rates. The peso which had been quoted at 40.75 pence in 1890-1891, had declined to 26.21 pence in 1895-1896, and down still further to 19.68 pence in 1902-1903. This dramatic decline had greatly increased the interest paid on the nation's debt, since it was payable in foreign currency.[35]

---

[34] Report of the Council of the Corporation of Foreign Bondholders (London, 1899), 258.

[35] Turlington, Mexico and Her Foreign Creditors, 221 fn.

Limantour attempted to stabilize the peso by establishing, as of May 1, 1905, a gold exchange standard. The peso was to be represented by 75 centigrams of gold. The silver peso was retained as legal tender, but had attributed to it the same value in gold. A special fund was created in order to maintain parity of foreign exchange value between the gold and the silver peso.[36]

Foreign involvement in Mexico's development is perhaps best exemplified by railway growth. By the turn of the century all important Mexican cities were connected by rail lines. Approximately 8,500 miles of track had been laid, most of it by competing foreign companies. Fearing that a merger was pending between the American interests controlling Mexico's two principal railway systems--the Mexican National Railway Company and the Central Railroad of Mexico, Limantour took decisive action to prevent the consolidation, which he believed would give the owners of the merged line too great an influence on Mexico's economy.

To prevent the merger, he authorized the purchase of nine million pesos in debentures of a line which the Mexican National was attempting to take over. He then exchanged these securities along with $4.5 million in cash with Speyer & Company, the New York investment house, for a controlling interest in the Mexican National line. With this move Liman-

_____

[36] Ibid., 233-234.

tour shrewdly had sidetracked a merger which might not have been in Mexico's best interest. Later, in 1909, he caused the government to acquire the Mexican Central and merge it with the Mexican National, in part to prevent one of the American railway systems from gaining control of the line.[37]

Stability and Limantour's financial wizardry rendered Mexico a haven for foreign investment. Only the panic of 1907 threatened Mexico's financial outlook. The large interest payments the nation was obliged to make annually and the profits going to foreign investors could be met only as long as new foreign investments continued to be made in Mexico and the country's balance of trade remained favorable. The panic of 1907 jolted American and European markets and produced a widespread lack of confidence that had temporary but detrimental impact on Mexico's economy.

By 1910, Mexico's total obligations to foreigners (direct or contingent) stood at approximately 450 million pesos. Net annual revenues amounted to at least 100 million pesos. Although Mexico's public debt was almost totally held by foreigners, there was little or no anxiety on the part of the government or the bondholders. With the approach of the centennial of the abortive Hidalgo rebellion of 1810, it appeared that most of the outstanding bonds in the hands of

---

[37] Ibid., 238-240.

foreigners were likely to be converted once again into new bonds with a lower interest rate. This was a reflection of Mexico's new status in the financial world.[38]

Limantour successfully negotiated in 1910 a ₤22.2 million loan at four percent intended exclusively for the redemption of the 1899 five percent bonds. This loan was placed with a syndicate composed of American, German, English, French and Mexican bankers. The loan undoubtedly represented the apex of Porfirian credit.[39]

Despite the almost miraculous transformation of Mexico from insolvency to fiscal respectability in only three decades, there were deep-rooted, fundamental flaws in the Mexican system. The increasingly uneven distribution of land was a potential source of unrest. At the time of independence Mexico had approximately 20,000 farms. In 1900 the number of farms had remained unchanged, while the population had more than doubled. Throughout the Díaz era land was concentrated in fewer and fewer hands. In 1894 Díaz had established a land registry which enabled *hacienda* owners to confiscate land of nearby Indians lacking formal titles. The policies of Díaz were so supportive of large landowners that by 1910 only 3,000 families owned a full one-half of the nation's land. Some 95 percent of the people working the

---

[38] Bazant, *La deuda exterior*, 163-179.
[39] Wynne, *State Insolvency*, 56-57.

land owned none of it; 85 percent of the cultivated land was in the hands of foreigners. In Baja California four individuals owned almost 30 million acres.[40]

This disproportionate distribution of land fostered widespread popular frustration. But oppression and peonage alone would not have led to revolution. It was the subjugation of hundreds of thousands of impoverished industrial workers and miners that combined with the feudal agrarian system to provide the foundation for revolution. By 1910 Mexican industry and mining were dominated by foreign capital. American interests alone had invested approximately 500 million pesos in Mexican properties. British and French capital, to the extent of some 100 million pesos, also were important to Mexican industrial expansion. Only about 30 million pesos came to this sector of the economy from Mexican sources.[41]

As the work force grew in geometric proportions and foreign investors reaped huge profits, the lot of industrial workers deteriorated. With a seven-day work week averaging

---

[40] Victor Alba, Horizon Concise History of Mexico (New York, 1973), 116; Frank Tannenbaum, Mexico: The Struggle for Peace and Bread (New York, 1960), 140-141.

[41] Marvin Bernstein, The Mexican Mining Industry, 1890-1950: A Study of the Interaction of Politics, Economics, and Technology (Albany, 1966), 72-77; Alba, Horizon History, 116.

12.5 hours per day under the most trying conditions, widespread workers' resentment festered beneath the surface of Díaz' superficially progressive society. Leaderless and inarticulate, the masses of poor Mexicans could do nothing to bring about reforms.

When in 1910 the aging dictator once again had himself reelected to the presidency for "the welfare of the nation," the politically ambitious upperclass Mexicans, who had been systematically excluded from participation in the government, began blatantly to plan revolution. Francisco I. Madero, who had been fraudulently defeated by Díaz in the election and was now in Texas, declared the election to be null and void and proclaimed himself the provisional president of Mexico. From the United States, Madero called for armed revolution. Returning to Mexico, he secured the support of other wealthy, liberal Mexicans. Together they succeeded quickly in organizing the masses who rallied to Madero's cause. His promise of land redistribution attracted millions of peons.[42]

---

[42] Among the best overviews of Madero and his role in the coming of the revolution are Charles C. Cumberland, The Mexican Revolution: Genesis Under Madero (Austin, 1952), and Stanley E. Ross, Francisco I. Madero: Apostle of Mexican Democracy (New York, 1955). Madero's political ideology is examined at length in James Cockcroft, Intellectual Precursors of the Mexican Revolution, 1900-1913 (Austin, 1968).

Madero's success was remarkable as was the haste with which Díaz yielded. By May 1911, Madero's revolutionary forces had triumphed. Francisco de la Barra was chosen provisional president until Madero could be elected in November 1911. Almost immediately after taking office Madero negotiated a $10 million loan through Speyer & Company in order to establish his government.[43] Unfortunately, the revolutionary tide once released was impossible to control. To the radicals Madero appeared too moderate--the revolution had whetted appetites for fundamental change. On the other side of the political spectrum, the large landowners were fearful of attempts at land reform, the military were offended by their limited role in the overthrow of Díaz, and the entrepreneurial class (domestic and foreign) sensed that their monopolistic position was in jeopardy.[44]

Madero found it costly to control all these dissenting elements. By September 1912 he was compelled to begin negotiations for a second loan. Before these negotiations could reach fruition, Madero was overthrown and murdered in February 1913 by a rightist coup d'état led by General Victoriano Huerta.

Although the United States never granted recognition

---

[43]Turlington, Mexico and Her Foreign Creditors, 247.

[44]Charles C. Cumberland, Mexican Revolution: The Constitutionalist Years (Austin, 1972), 3-10.

to the Huerta government, American Ambassador Henry Lane Wilson immediately established informal relations with the new administration. It is likely, despite his claims to the contrary, that Wilson also doomed Madero when he told Huerta that he should do with the imprisoned President, "whatever was in the best interest of Mexico." Soon thereafter Madero was murdered.[45]

Wilson, an old-line reactionary diplomat, was angered that the Madero revolution had jeopardized the peace and stability of the Díaz decades which had proven so conducive to American investment in Mexico. The conservative Huerta regime held promise of restoring a Porfirian order. Wilson functioned as a catalyst for this restoration. Important bankers in Europe and the United States reportedly were pressuring their governments to recognize Huerta. It was generally assumed that the incoming administration of Woodrow Wilson would routinely grant recognition.[46]

But recognition was not to come. An embryonic anti-Huerta counter-coup led by Venustiano Carranza placed Huerta's government in jeopardy. The Wilson administration failed to acknowledge Huerta. On the contrary, Wilson recalled Ambassador Wilson and sent John Lind to Mexico City

---

[45]Henry Lane Wilson, Diplomatic Episodes in Mexico, Belgium and Chile (Garden City, N.Y., 1927), 273-286.

[46]The checkered history of American recognition policy toward Mexico is carefully examined in Stuart A. MacCorkle, The American Policy of Recognition Toward Mexico (Baltimore, 1933).

as a confidential agent to attempt to convince Huerta to allow the election of a constitutional government that the United States could recognize.[47] A large international loan, desperately needed to bring order to the nation, fell through when Carranza warned that if he was successful he would not honor obligations entered into by Huerta. Huerta blamed the United States for his complex problems.

Tensions, however, seemed to ease in June 1913, when a syndicate of French, German, English and American bankers led by the latter granted the Huerta government a six percent loan for L16 million maturing in 1923.[48] That same month the governments of Great Britain, Germany, France, Russia, Spain and Portugal recognized the Huerta government, and it was widely believed that Wilson was soon to follow.[49]

The continued success of Carranza's constitutionalists and the added pressures from the bands of guerillas led by Emiliano Zapata[50] in the south and Pancho Villa[51]

---

[47] Lind's efforts and experiences in Mexico are detailed in George M. Stephson, *John Lind of Minnesota* (Minneapolis, 1935), and Larry D. Hill, *Emissaries to a Revolution: Woodrow Wilson's Executive Agents in Mexico* (Baton Rouge, 1973).

[48] Wynne, *State Insolvency*, 60-63.

[49] Turlington, *Mexico and Her Foreign Creditors*, 251.

[50] Zapata's role in the revolution is portrayed in John Womack, *Zapata and the Mexican Revolution* (New York, 1969).

[51] If read with caution Martin Luis Guzman's *Memoirs of Pancho Villa* (Austin, 1965), can be helpful. This autobiographical reconstruction is based on notes allegedly dictated by Villa and provides details of his life through 1915.

in the north proved costly to combat. The ₤16 million loan was inadequate to maintain the government and to put down the three-pronged rebellion. Huerta was forced to declare the Treasury bankrupt on January 13, 1914, with a decree that suspended for six months interest payments on both internal and foreign indebtedness.[52]

From that juncture Huerta's fall was but a matter of time. By spring 1914 only a few cities, including Mexico City and Veracruz, were under federal control. President Wilson had responded to the fraudulent election on October 26, 1913, by lifting the arms embargo he had imposed on all sides in the civil war two months earlier. Henceforth anti-Huerta revolutionaries could purchase arms in the United States. In April 1914 an incident occurred between Huerta's troops and some American marines. An American naval officer made an absurd demand that Mexico demonstrate its contrition by saluting the American flag. Mexico refused. Wilson sent several naval vessels to blockade Veracruz harbor. While steadfastly maintaining his desire for peace, Wilson took additional steps which exacerbated the insignificant episode. He went before a joint session of Congress and asked for authority to use the armed forces to obtain redress. The naval and military branches were ordered to

---

[52] No further payments were made on the foreign debt until January 1, 1923; these were the result of the Lamont-de la Huerta Agreement. "Memorandum on the Public Debt of Mexico," May 20, 1928, Morrow Papers.

make preparations for possible war. In order to avoid a naval conflict with a German ship heading for Veracruz with arms for Huerta, Wilson ordered the marines to land briefly at that port city. The Mexicans resisted vehemently. This proved to be a serious misjudgment, for even Carranza protested this violation of Mexican territory.[53]

Only a timely offer to mediate by the Washington envoys of Argentina, Brazil and Chile prevented an immediate, more bloody confrontation. Yet for Wilson this mediation was only a ploy intended to bring about the removal of Huerta and his replacement by a provisional government of constitutionalists. While the negotiations dragged on, the Carranza forces rolled on toward Mexico City. Carranza foiled Wilson's scheme by making clear to the American president that United States mediation in the civil war itself was unwelcome and that the economic and social reconstruction of Mexico would be accomplished in accordance with Carranza's plans.[54]

On July 15, 1914, Huerta resigned. A month later on August 20, Carranza assumed the executive power which he

---

[53] The episode is detailed in Robert E. Quirk, An Affair of Honor: Woodrow Wilson and the Occupation of Veracruz (Lexington, 1962), and in Jack Sweetman, The Landing at Veracruz: 1914 (Annapolis, 1968). The best brief account of the Veracruz incident and its impact on Mexican-American relations can be found in Arthur Link, Woodrow Wilson and the Progressive Era (New York, 1954), 122-128.

[54] Cumberland, Mexican Revolution: The Constitutionalist Years, 294.

was to hold for almost six years. It might have been expected that Wilson would acknowledge a government which had come to power, at least in part, because of policies pursued by the United States. But Wilson did not grant *de facto* recognition to the new government for 15 months.

In the interim Wilson made an ill-conceived decision to support the ambitious *vaquero*, Pancho Villa, against the new Carranza government. The crude but charismatic Villa had appeared inclined to follow American wishes and thus seemed less dangerous than the independent Carranza. An ill-fated convention, inspired by American diplomacy, was held at Aguascalientes, beginning on October 10, 1914. Although the primary objective of this meeting was to get both Villa and Carranza to step aside so that a moderate could unite both factions, it soon became apparent that Villa, with the assistance of Zapata, had gained control of the gathering. When the convention elected a Villa stooge, Eulalio Gutiérrez, as president on November 3, 1914, Carranza balked and declared war on the usurpers.[55]

Once again the United States supported Villa. The bloody civil war that followed was dominated by General Alvaro Obregón, a staunch supporter of Carranza who, from January to September 15, pursued and defeated the Villistas as they retreated north. This turn of events led the

---

[55]*Ibid.*, 170-178.

Wilson administration to declare its strict neutrality and, quite self-righteously, to insist that Mexico be left to solve its own domestic problems. No doubt Wilson's neutral stance was greatly influenced by the real danger that the United States might soon be obliged to declare war on Germany because of that nation's refusal to stop submarine warfare against merchant shipping.[56]

Obregón's dramatic successes forced Wilson to grant *de facto* recognition to the Carranza government on October 19, 1915. Villa responded in January 1916 by massacring 16 Americans at Santa Ysabel and then, in March, crossed into New Mexico where he staged a bloody raid on Columbus before returning to safety south of the border.[57]

Wilson, preparing for a second presidential campaign, at first hesitated to send troops to Mexico despite a public outcry for such action. As pressure from many quarters mounted, Wilson was compelled to negotiate an agreement with the Carranza government which allowed the United States to pursue Villa's raiders into Mexico. Although Carranza would soon repudiate this accord, a Punitive Expedition, composed of well over 5,000 men, under Brigadier General John J. Pershing crossed into Mexico in futile pursuit of

---

[56] Link, *Wilson and the Progressive Era*, 132-133.

[57] A detailed report of the two episodes is found in Clarence C. Clendenen, *Blood on the Border: The United States Army and the Mexican Irregulars* (New York, 1969), 197-210.

Villa. The cunning guerilla leader proved to be most elusive, meanwhile tempers flared on both sides of the Rio Grande.

Pershing drove deeper and deeper into Mexico, much to the chagrin of Carranza who soon was forced to demand American withdrawal from his country.[58] The political futures of both presidents depended on their not losing face in this episode. Wilson replied that the federal government appeared unwilling or unable to control the Villistas and that it was up to the United States to protect its citizens from slaughter. After months of confrontation, crisis and occasional conflict, growing concern over imminent war with Germany caused Wilson to withdraw the American troops on January 27, 1917.[59]

The revolution and civil war proved costly to Mexico both in terms of expenditures needed to restore law and order and because of the inability of the Mexican economy to function at anything approaching a normal pace. From the outset of the revolution, Carranza and the other revolutionary leaders used hastily printed fiat currency with which to purchase needed supplies. This paper money issued in

---

[58] P. Edward Haley, Revolution and Intervention: The Diplomacy of Taft and Wilson with Mexico, 1910-1917 (Cambridge, 1970), 197-199.

[59] Link, Wilson and the Progressive Era, 140-144.

huge quantities--about 1.25 billion pesos--caused a spectacular inflation which by the end of 1916 resulted in the collapse of the monetary system. The paper peso had become worthless.[60] Unable to secure a foreign loan, Carranza damaged the Mexican economy still further in December 1916, when he appropriated approximately 54 million pesos, the cash reserves of Mexico's banks. Bank notes then ceased to be legal currency.[61]

In December 1916 Carranza used the prestige he had accrued as a result of his firm stance against American intervention to call a constituent assembly. Although he had assumed that the product of this meeting would be only a revision of the existing constitution, the assembly drafted a new constitution modeled after the one of the United States but containing some innovative provisions reflecting the revolutionary spirit that had swept Mexico. Probably the most controversial provision of the 1917 Constitution was Article 27. This article declared:

> The Nation shall have at all times the right to impose on private property such limitations as the public interest may demand as well as the right to regulate the development of natural resources, which are susceptible of appropriation, in order to conserve them and equitably to distribute the public wealth.[62]

---

[60] An excellent analysis of the collapse of Mexico's monetary system is Edwin W. Kemmerer, Inflation and Revolution: Mexico's Experience, 1912-1917 (Princeton, 1940).

[61] Wynne, State Insolvency, 64-65.

[62] Article 27 is quoted in full in Turlington, Mexico and Her Foreign Creditors, 270 fn.

It was this provision, with its clear threat of confiscation of foreign held properties, which was to arouse the anxieties and consternation of foreign investors and governments worldwide.[63]

The new constitution was approved and promulgated on February 5, 1917. The next month, on March 11, a new Congress and a President--Carranza--were chosen in accordance with the provisions of the constitution. Two days later the United States granted de jure recognition to the constitutional government by dispatching Ambassador Henry P. Fletcher to Mexico City. The new constitution went into effect on May 1, 1917.

Mexico's dire fiscal plight endured. No payments had been made on the foreign debt since 1913, and very little progress was being made toward financial stability. Article 27 of the constitution was so repugnant to many foreigners that they were strongly disinclined to grant new loans to a government pursuing a policy of confiscation of private property. The brief but dangerous willingness of Carranza to entertain the blatant overtures of Germany further alienated potential creditors.

---

[63] For discussions of the origins of Article 27 and foreign reaction to it, see Pastor Roaix, *Genesis de los articulos 27 y 123 de la Constitución Politica de 1917* (Mexico City, 1959), and John P. Bullington, "Problems of International Law in the Mexican Constitution of 1917," *American Journal of International Law*, XXI (October 1927), 685-705.

CHAPTER II

INTERNATIONAL COMMITTEE OF BANKERS ON MEXICO

The major investment banking firms of the United States and western Europe viewed with obvious anxiety the almost continuous deterioration of Mexican stability which followed the murder of Madero. Although they had initially looked favorably upon the Huerta government, it soon became apparent that he would not be able to keep the Mexican economy on an even keel while fighting a three-front civil war. The bankers attempted to provide Huerta with access to new credit but Wilson's steadfast refusal to recognize the new government and the successes of Carranza, Villa and Zapata rendered this approach impracticable.

Carranza's accession to the presidency did not alleviate these anxieties, since Villa and Zapata were unwilling to acknowledge his authority; meanwhile, the civil war continued. Late in 1915 a committee was created in London under the chairmanship of Vivian H. Smith, a partner in Morgan, Grenfell & Company, to represent British holders of Mexican securities in default. Smith's firm had underwritten a portion of the Mexican loans of 1899, 1910 and 1913. Although this committee achieved little in terms of commitments from Carranza, it did establish informal relations with American and French investment banks with similar interests. These ties paved the way for the formation of the International Committee of Bankers on Mexico which formally came into being in February 1919.[1]

It had been hoped that the armistice ending the Great War would enable the United States to resolve amicably the long-standing tensions between the Carranza and Wilson governments. Hopefully Carranza's neutrality in the war could be forgotten in the United States and the unhappy American intervention in Mexico would become less important to the Mexicans with the passing of time. Unfortunately, such optimism was unjustified.

There were still powerful forces in the United States advocating the use of force to protect American rights and property in Mexico. Carranza had demonstrated abundantly that he could not guarantee the protection of foreign property. Quite to the contrary, his social and economic reform policies jeopardized it further. Although he intimated that Article 27 of the 1917 Constitution would not be applied retroactively, American oil firms were denied permission to drill new wells unless they relinquished their claims to subsoil rights on their pre-1917 properties.[2] Lands belonging to foreign holders were gradually being confiscated and

---

[1] Wynne, State Insolvency, 66.

[2] Clifford W. Trow, "Woodrow Wilson and the Mexican Interventionist Movement of 1919," Journal of American History, LVIII (June 1971), 61.

distributed to the peons in order to reestablish the ejidos (communal holdings), with bonds of very questionable value issued in exchange.

In December 1918, several of the affected interests organized the National Association for the Protection of American Rights in Mexico. This organization functioned as a lobbying group to bring pressure upon the Wilson administration to take a harder line toward Carranza and hopefully to intervene to protect foreign property.[3]

Within the administration the viewpoint of this group was generally shared by Wilson's Secretary of State, Robert Lansing, who had long since lost patience with Mexico. Greatly influenced by American Ambassador to Mexico, Henry P. Fletcher, Lansing formulated policies in the State Department that were clearly contrary to the objectives Wilson espoused. Fletcher and George T. Summerlin, chargé d'affaires in Mexico City, both argued for the use of force to protect American lives and property. Wilson, however, would not countenance armed intervention. He viewed the Pershing expedition as a legitimate form of diplomatic interposition (allowed under international law), but drew a firm line against the kinds of actions being called for by Lansing and in many other quarters.[4]

---

[3] Joseph S. Tulchin, The Aftermath of War: World War I and United States Policy Toward Latin America (New York, 1971), 73.

[4] Ibid., 72-73.

Also influential in the movement for firm action was Senator Albert B. Fall, who used his Subcommittee on Foreign Relations to keep public opinion stirred up against Mexico. This stance would endear Fall to the petroleum interests. Unfortunately, Wilson was occupied with the resolution of European problems and was unable to keep a close check on these dissenting elements within the United States.

Although the United States was to have three Secretaries of State in a thirteen-month span (Lansing, Bainbridge Colby, and Charles Evans Hughes), continuity was provided by the presence of Frank L. Polk in the State Department throughout this period. Polk was opposed to military intervention and in his roles as Undersecretary of State and Acting Secretary, while Lansing was with Wilson in Paris, and interim Secretary between Lansing's resignation and Colby's confirmation, Polk functioned as a moderating force. It was Polk who acted as a liaison for the Department with the International Committee of Bankers on Mexico.

On October 4, 1918, Thomas W. Lamont of J.P. Morgan & Company conferred with Polk concerning the feasibility of forming a committee to "look after international investment interests in Mexico." Lamont informed the State Department that British and French interests had for some time been urging the Morgan firm to head such a committee. It was agreed that Fletcher would sound out Carranza to determine if he would cooperate with such an undertaking.[5]

Several months passed with no word from Fletcher. Lamont began to pressure the State Department for a decision on the committee claiming that other houses "of less weight and influence" might form their own committee, with the implication that this would not be in the best interest of all concerned.[6] On January 7, 1919, Polk responded that Ambassador Fletcher had recently expressed the opinion that it was "inadvisable to broach the subject to President Carranza" but that he [Polk] approved the organization of the committee. It was to be composed of representatives of leading American banking firms and their British and French counterparts. The approval included the stipulation that "Americans would retain the direction of the proposed Committee, which would comprise substantial international groups designed to represent practically all of Mexico's creditors and capable of dealing with the situation as a whole."[7]

Six weeks later, on February 23, 1919, the formal announcement of the formation of the Committee was made. In the interim preliminary contacts were made between the Car-

---

[5]Frank L. Polk to Thomas W. Lamont, October 8, 1918, Drawer 81, Frank L. Polk Papers, Yale University Library, New Haven, Connecticut (Hereafter cited as Polk Papers); Lamont to Polk, November 18, 1918, FRUS 1919, II, 644-645.

[6]Lamont to Polk, December 13, 1918, ibid., 645-646.

[7]Polk to J.P. Morgan & Co., January 7, 1919, ibid., 646-647.

ranza government and the Morgan firm. On February 10, 1919, a meeting was held in New York between Raphael Nieto, Mexican Acting Minister of Finance, and Thomas Cochran, a Morgan partner.[8] Nieto stated that President Carranza desired to resume the payment of interest on Mexico's debts. He presented for discussion a preliminary proposal for a Mexican financial reorganization. Cochran expressed doubt that the proposal outlined was feasible since it called for an arbitrary 50 percent reduction in the outstanding debt, which he believed bondholders would not approve, and for an additional loan of approximately $100 million, which Cochran felt could not be made without guarantees from the United States government.[9]

Cochran agreed to study the proposals further, discuss them with other American bankers and with French and British interests and then to broach the subject with the State Department.[10]

Two weeks later an announcement in the press formally revealed the formation of the Committee composed of ten Americans, with five British and five French representatives.

---

[8]Lamont was not available, having sailed for Paris where he was an adviser to Wilson on European financial matters.

[9]Minutes of "Informal Conference on the Financial Position of Mexico," February 10, 1919, Box 192, Thomas W. Lamont Papers, Baker Library, Harvard University, Boston, Massachusetts (Hereafter cited as Lamont Papers).

[10]Ibid.

J.P. Morgan was named chairman.[11] The goal of the Committee was the protection of holders of "securities of the Mexican Republic and of the various railway systems of Mexico, and generally of such other enterprises as have their field of action in Mexico."[12]

---

[11] Morgan soon yielded the chairmanship to Lamont. The American section of the Committee at the outset was made up of J.P. Morgan, John J. Mitchell of the Illinois Trust and Savings Bank (Chicago), Walter T. Rosen of Landenburg, Thalmann & Company (New York), Mortimer L. Schiff of Kuhn, Loeb & Company (New York), James A. Stillman of National City Bank (New York), James N. Wallace of the Central-Union Trust Company (New York), Albert H. Wiggin of Chase National Bank (New York), Robert Winsor of Kidder, Peabody & Company (Boston). The British section was composed of Vivian H. Smith of Morgan, Grenfell & Company (London), Laurence Currie of Glyn, Mills, Currie & Company (London), Clarendon Hyde of S. Pearson & Sons, Ltd. (London), Vincent W. Yorke of the Mexican Railway Company, Ltd. (London), and E.R. Peacock, Chairman of the bondholders committee of the Mexican Tramways and the Mexican Light & Power Company (London). The French section consisted of William d'Eichthal of Mirabaud & Co. (Paris), Georges Heine of Banque de l'Union Parisienne, Jacques Kulp of the Banque de Paris et des Pays Bas (Paris), Joseph Simon of the Commission for the Protection of French Holders of Mexican Securities and André Honorat of the same commission. E.R. Tinker was named secretary of the American section (later replaced by Vernon Munroe) and Ira H. Patchin was appointed assistant secretary. The membership of the three sections changed frequently in the next decade. Very few individuals remained on the Committee for more than a few years.

[12] New York Times, February 24, 1919; The Commercial and Financial Chronicle, CVI (March 1, 1919), 824-825.

Soon after the announcement Carranza made known his approval of the Committee and sent Nieto to see Morgan on March 7, 1919. Nieto indicated that this was the favorable time for action. He stated that Carranza felt that Wilson was more likely to be reasonable toward Mexico than a new administration because his policies had met with such dramatic failure in the past. Morgan made clear to Nieto that all thoughts of debt repudiation in regard to the Díaz issue of 1899 and the 1913 Huerta debt must be abandoned, and that any new financing would undoubtedly require guarantees from the United States government. Carranza previously had objected to this, but, Morgan said, had to be "educated up to it." Morgan pointed out that the offerings of 1899 and 1913 were secured. While postponement of service on these issues might be necessary until Mexico's income increased, repudiation was unacceptable.[13]

The first meeting of the American section of the International Committee took place on March 13, 1919. Three subcommittees were formed to study the questions of public debt, railways and industry, respectively. It was agreed that the State Department should be consulted regarding the advisability of including Dutch and Swiss members to the Committee, since significant amounts of Mexican securities were held

---

[13]Minutes of "Conference on Refinancing of Mexico," March 7, 1919, Box 192, Lamont Papers.

in those nations. If excluded, they might seek to protect themselves to the detriment of the Committee.[14]

Although the Committee continued to work under the direction of the State Department to arrive at a plan acceptable to all parties, events in Mexico negated their efforts. An extraordinary session of the Mexican Congress meeting in May 1919 failed to approve the assignment of revenues for an anticipated American loan. Additionally, no legislation was enacted to modify the constitutional provisions allowing the confiscation of oil lands.[15]

Throughout 1919 raids by Villistas into the United States exacerbated an already tense situation. When Polk went to Paris in mid-July 1919 to assist Wilson in the peace negotiations, Lansing and Fletcher took over the execution of policy toward Mexico. Neither was tolerant of Mexican deviance from expected international norms. Almost immediately a new, harder line was taken by the Department.[16]

In October 1919 American Consular Agent at Puebla,

---

[14] Minutes of "Meeting of the American Group of the International Committee of Bankers on Mexico," March 13, 1919, Box 192, ibid.

[15] Turlington, Mexico and Her Foreign Creditors, 278. In July 1919 Carranza allowed the issuance of provisional drilling permits but with conditions that were virtually impossible for the oil companies to meet. Henry P. Fletcher to Polk, July 24, 1919, Drawer 81, Polk Papers.

[16] Tulchin, The Aftermath of War, 74.

William O. Jenkins, was kidnapped by rebels who apparently desired to demonstrate the inability of the Carranza government to protect foreigners. Although this was merely a token action and Jenkins was released six days later, public opinion in the United States was brought to fever pitch in favor of intervention. A resolution was introduced in the Senate calling for such action. Jenkins' release failed to ease tensions since he was soon arrested by the Carranza government and charged with faking the kidnapping in conspiracy with the rebels in order to embarrass the government.[17]

American reaction to this new offense was swift. On November 20, 1919, Lansing instructed Summerlin to demand Jenkins' immediate release.[18] On November 28, Lansing informed the Mexican Ambassador, Ignacio Bonillas, that severance of diplomatic relations was a real possibility and that such a break would "almost inevitably mean war."[19]

Tensions were further heightened when the Mexican army began seizing oil wells drilled without government permits.[20]

---

[17] The episode is detailed in Charles C. Cumberland, "The Jenkins Case and Mexican-American Relations," Hispanic American Historical Review, XXXI (November 1951), 586-607.

[18] Robert Lansing to George T. Summerlin, November 20, 1919, FRUS 1919, II, 578-590. See also David Glaser, "1919: William Jenkins, Robert Lansing, and the Mexican Interlude," Southwestern Historical Quarterly, LXXIV (January 1971), 337-356.

[19] Edward M. House Diary, December 27, 1919, Edward M. House Papers, Yale University Library, New Haven, Conn.

[20] Trow, "Woodrow Wilson," 61.

Then Luis Cabrera, Minister of Finance, declared that before Mexico would resume payment on its debts it would await the outcome of current world developments in order to see which nations in the postwar period would repudiate their debts or reduce their obligations "to figures compatible with their income."[21]

Senator Fall, with the support of Lansing and Fletcher, introduced a resolution in the Senate on December 3, 1919, calling for an immediate break of diplomatic relations with Mexico and demanding the use of force to protect American lives and property.[22] When the ailing Wilson finally became aware of the critical state of Mexican-American relations on December 5, he ordered the State Department to ask the Senate to postpone action on the Fall resolution. That same day Carranza released Jenkins. The resolution died in the Committee on Foreign Relations three days later.[23] This antagonized Fall and was an important contributing factor in the resignations of Lansing and Fletcher in February 1920.

Later in December the intimate relationship between the International Committee and the State Department was

---

[21] U.S. Senate, Committee on Foreign Relations, 66th Cong., 2nd Sess., Investigation of Mexican Affairs (2 vols., Washington, D.C., 1920), II, 3301.

[22] Trow, "Woodrow Wilson," 64; Manuel A. Machado Jr. and James T. Judge, "Tempest in a Teapot? The Mexican-United States Intervention Crisis of 1919," Southwestern Historical Quarterly, LXXIV (July 1970), 1-23.

[23] Trow, "Woodrow Wilson," 46.

once again reaffirmed when Lamont, on behalf of the Committee, suggested to the Department that it would be petty for the American section of the Committee to be enlarged merely because Swiss and Dutch members were added to assure that the American membership always was equal to the combined number of the other nations. He acknowledged that it was "already understood and agreed" that "effective control of policy [was] to be maintained by the Department of State."[24] The Department responded that the details of the composition of the Committee would be left to Lamont's judgment, "provided always that the effective control of policy remains in our hands."[25]

The final year of Wilson's second term was an eventful one for Mexican-American relations and for the International Committee. Wilson had long viewed Lansing with distrust, with good reason.[26] Lansing's covert and unholy relationship with Wilson's avowed Republican enemies on the Foreign Relations Committee with regard to Mexico did little to alleviate those feeling. Wilson wrote to Lansing on February 7, 1920, accusing him of disloyalty and usurpation. The Secretary resigned on February 13. Fletcher tendered his resig-

---

[24] Lamont to Fletcher, December 23, 1919, FRUS 1919, II, 648-649.

[25] Fletcher to Lamont, December 27, 1919, ibid., 649.

[26] Arthur S. Link, Wilson the Diplomatist (Chicago, 1957), 26-27; Daniel M. Smith, Aftermath of War: Bainbridge Colby and Wilsonian Diplomacy, 1920-1921 (Philadelphia, 1970), 5-6.

nation along with Lansing, having totally despaired as to the possibility of firm action against Mexico. Wilson then blocked the appointment of another interventionist, George Summerlin, as Assistant Secretary of State.[27]

Polk acted as interim Secretary of State from Lansing's resignation until the appointment of Colby as Secretary on March 23, 1920. Colby was an attorney of unquestionable personal loyalty to Wilson but totally lacking in diplomatic experience. Wilson was determined to enjoy at least one year in the White House with a loyal man heading the State Department.[28]

By the time of Colby's appointment events in Mexico were once again rushing towards civil war. Carranza, unable to succeed himself constitutionally, chose Ambassador Bonillas as his successor. The opposition party selected General Obregón, who enjoyed the support of the military. Obregónistas accused Carranza of attempting to impose a president upon the people and viciously attacked Bonillas as a "gringo" who had been so long in the United States as to have lost understanding and appreciation for Mexican problems.[29]

---

[27] Tulchin, The Aftermath of War, 77.

[28] Wilson to Polk, February 24, 1920, Drawer 89, Polk Papers.

[29] Cumberland, Mexican Revolution: The Constitutionalist Years, 406.

Obregón found it increasingly difficult to conduct a presidential campaign because of Carranza's blatant harassment. Popular opinion was steadily mounting behind Obregón. Then Carranza took a series of oppressive actions against Obregón's home state--Sonora--an anti-Carranza hot-bed, which brought that state to the brink of rebellion. Determined to have his way, Carranza ordered federal troops into Sonora, ostensibly to control the then placid Yaqui indians. Adolfo de la Huerta, Governor of the state, protested and Carranza replied with arrogance that if Sonora believed its rights were being violated it could appeal to the Supreme Court. On April 9, 1920, Sonora severed its relations with the national government. Other states quickly followed and full-scale civil war raged again. Most federal troops deserted Carranza, and by May 7 he was forced to abandon Mexico City. On May 20 the President was caught and slain. De la Huerta was named president of the provisional government.[30]

Although the plan under discussion between the International Committee and the Carranza government for the resumption of payments on the foreign debt were abandoned at the time of the Sonora rebellion, there was general optimism in the United States that a new government would prove

---

[30] Ibid., 408-413.

more reasonable than Carranza had been. On September 5, 1920, a constitutional election was held and, as anticipated, Obregón won handily. Yet even before he took office on December 1, indications had been given that the new regime appreciated Mexico's financial responsibilities. De la Huerta declared, on October 22, that Mexico would honor all its debts and had no intention of confiscating property.[31] A series of meetings between Undersecretary of State Norman H. Davis and various Mexican representatives in October 1920 led Colby and Wilson to believe that Mexico was not insensitive to American concerns.[32]

In anticipation of improved relations and the opportunities this would present for final settlement of the foreign debt, and aware that the November election would probably bring Harding to the White House, Lamont again contacted the State Department in order to reaffirm the unique relationship between the Committee and the Department. This move seemed necessary, in view of the personnel changes within the department. Lamont reminded Davis that it was essential "that if the general situation of Mexico with reference to her outside creditors is to be discussed, then this Committee is the proper medium for such discussions.... if any

---

[31]Turlington, Mexico and Her Foreign Creditors, 280-281.
[32]Smith, Aftermath of War, 111-113.

one is to be sent to Mexico, this International Committee should preeminently be represented."[33]

Davis agreed that the Committee should play an important role in any new efforts to resolve the Mexican debt question. He informed Wilson of the relationship of the Committee to the State Department and suggested to the President that Lamont head a delegation to Mexico City to initiate discussions with the Obregón government. The British and French interests were pressuring the American group for an immediate delegation to Mexico, and it was feared by Lamont that they might go there without the American representatives.[34] Wilson recommended that the trip be discouraged pending a decision on recognition.[35]

Of fundamental interest to all parties--the new Mexican government, the Wilson administration, the International Committee and all foreign holders of Mexican property--was the question of American recognition of Obregón. Recognition had been withheld from Huerta in 1913 largely on moral grounds. He had come to power through illegal means, allowed the legitimately elected president to be murdered and then made a travesty of the electoral process. Obregón had circumven-

---

[33] Lamont to Norman H. Davis, September 28, 1920, FRUS 1920, III, 230-231.

[34] Davis to Wilson, November 2, 1920, ibid., 234-235.

[35] Wilson to Colby, November 5, 1920, ibid., 236.

ted these moral issues by quickly calling a democratic election which enabled Wilson to ignore the means by which power was taken from Carranza. Yet the United States had learned a lesson from the premature recognition of Carranza. Now, before recognition would be bestowed, it was necessary that Obregón demonstrate unequivocally his good intentions. Colby had announced on October 13, 1920, that recognition would be granted when a Mixed Claims Commission was established, the foreign debt was acknowledged and the apparently retroactive provisions of the Constitution were satisfactorily clarified, amended or hopefully abrogated.[36] Few believed that these conditions would present long-term obstacles to recognition.

Wilson had settled upon "nonrecognition" as a peaceful alternative to the armed intervention argument he had firmly rejected a year earlier. He was prepared to use the leverage afforded by the temporary withholding of recognition in order to obtain the desired concessions from Obregón but made clear to the State Department and Congress that intervention was one instrument of diplomacy he was unwilling to use again. To a degree this limited the Department in its efforts to force Mexico to resolve the differences between the two nations in the manner desired by the United

---

[36] New York Times, October 30, 1920.

States.[37]

In the last months of the Wilson administration various individuals and groups desirous of using recognition as a club against Mexican recalcitrance vehemently voiced their concerns that an early recognition would leave Obregón with no incentive to honor his promises as president-elect. Colby and Wilson were besieged by land and oil interests and by Fall and other hard-liners in Congress. Undoubtedly these groups felt that President-elect Harding would be coming to office in a few months and that the Republicans would be more sensitive to the needs of business and investment interests.[38]

Obregón too apparently hoped that the Harding administration would bring a change from the Wilsonian policy of "watchful waiting."[39] Meanwhile the General hoped to free himself from the constraints imposed on him by a decade of anti-American sentiment. In apparent anticipation of better relations, Obregón sanctioned extending an invitation to Lamont. On February 7, 1921, Lamont was invited to visit Mexico for discussions of the means by which a settlement of outstanding financial questions could be reached.[40]

---

[37]Tulchin, The Aftermath of War, 77-78.

[38]Smith, Aftermath of War, 113-114.

[39]Ibid., 116.

[40]Commercial and Financial Chronicle, CX (February 12, 1921), 603-604.

Lamont consulted the State Department concerning the advisability of accepting Obregón's invitation on behalf of the Committee. The State Department "was very clear that I better not go quite yet," he reported later. He responded to the Mexican overture with a statement that while he welcomed the invitation, he must consult with the State Department and that he suspected that it would probably want the Committee to discuss the matter with the incoming Harding administration.[41]

In advising Lamont not to accept the invitation, the State Department was in agreement with the sentiments of Senator Fall. Fall wrote Lamont that he believed that "no American banking institution should enter into negotiations of any kind with Mexico, until Mexico had, in some way, or by some method, reached a settlement with the Government of the United States."[42]

So far as it concerned itself with Mexico, the Harding administration, in its early months, suffered from a basic difference of opinion between the President and Secretary of State Charles Evans Hughes. Harding was very interested in a quick resolution of the long-standing friction with Mexico. He encouraged numerous informal contacts with the

---

[41] Lamont to J. Ridgely Carter, February 9, 1921, Box 192, Lamont Papers.

[42] Fall to Lamont, February 11, 1921, Box 192, *ibid*.

Obregon government outside of normal diplomatic channels in order to ascertain the feasibility of opening new negotiations between the two nations. Hughes, on the other hand, objected to this approach and Harding yielded in the interest of harmony.[43]

Although Hughes believed that recognition was desirable for the normalization of relations between the two neighbors, he held property rights to be sacred and hence formulated a tough policy with Mexico. Hughes was influenced and supported in his firm stance by former Ambassador Fletcher, now Undersecretary of State, and by Summerlin, charge d'affaires in Mexico City. Both men continued to be staunch advocates of "big stick" diplomacy.[44]

Hughes was perfectly prepared to employ America's postwar position as the world's foremost creditor nation in order to achieve his diplomatic goals. Ironically, in implementing this approach to Mexican-American relations, Hughes adopted some distinctively Wilsonian objectives. He demanded, before recognition was granted, that Mexico sign a formal Treaty of Amity and Commerce including specific guaran-

---

[43] Robert K. Murray, The Harding Era (Minneapolis, 1969), 329.

[44] Tulchin, The Aftermath of War, 97.

tees regarding the property rights of Americans.[45] Like Wilson, Hughes wanted compensation for all American losses in Mexico since the fall of Díaz. Obregón refused to yield.[46]

The Republican administration was much more responsive to the International Committee than the Democrats had been. Hughes and Fletcher were in frequent contact with Lamont. When, early in June 1921, Obregón complained publicly that despite his good intentions his invitation to Lamont had not been accepted, Lamont wrote Hughes that his responsibilities as Acting Chairman dictated that he not delay much longer in accepting the invitation as long as the trip did not "interfere with the Department's handling of the political situation."[47]

Before the month was out, Lamont again wrote Hughes of his belief that it was "highly expedient" to respond to Obregón's invitation since information received by the Committee indicated that opposition to Obregón in Mexico was

---

[45]The text of the proposed treaty as submitted by Summerlin to Alberto Pani, Secretary for Foreign Relations, on May 27, 1921, is in Mexico, Secretaría de Relaciones Exteriores. La cuestión internacional mexicano-americana durante el gobierno del Gral. Don Alvaro Obregón (3rd ed., Mexico City, 1949), 16-25.

[46]Murray, The Harding Era, 329; N. Stephen Kane, "Bankers and Diplomats: The Diplomacy of the Dollar in Mexico, 1921-1924," Business History Review, LXVII (Autumn 1973), 336-337.

[47]Lamont to Charles Evans Hughes, June 9, 1921, Box 192, Lamont Papers.

mounting and such a gesture would bolster his position.[48] The implication was clear that the Obregón government was probably more desirable than what might follow in its wake, and in the absence of American recognition this token action by the Committee might prevent or postpone its downfall.

Hughes consented to the proposed trip, and it was agreed that Lamont would go to Mexico in early fall.[49] Before departing for the Mexican capital, Lamont and Hughes conferred at length as to the agenda for the discussions and the stance he should take with regard to the important issues. They agreed that Lamont would make clear to the Mexicans that no new loan could be floated as long as the government remained unrecognized by the United States, Britain and France.[50] Hughes was convinced of Lamont's capabilities and asked only that his discussion be "consistent with our [State Department] policy."[51] Since the Department and the International Committee shared common objectives--the protection of foreign property in Mexico and the restoration of stability south of the border--Hughes had no need for concern.

---

[48]Lamont to Hughes, June 27, 1921, Box 192, ibid.

[49]Hughes to Lamont, June 29, 1921, FRUS 1921, II, 487-488.

[50]Lamont to Hughes, September 2, 1921 and September 13, 1921, ibid., 498-499.

[51]Memorandum, dated August 15, 1921, Box 195, Lamont Papers.

Just prior to Lamont's departure for Mexico a snag developed which cast a shadow over the upcoming negotiations. Since mid-1921 representatives of the petroleum interests had been vigorously opposing an increase in the oil export tax, which was intended to raise new funds to be used for the resumption of interest payments on the external debt. Their objections were so powerfully offered that de la Huerta, Minister of Finance, compromised by agreeing that the tax could be paid with Mexican government bonds which were then selling at less than 40 percent of their face value. It was expected that a syndicate of American bankers would purchase quantities of the securities for the oil companies at a generous profit for themselves. This fanciful proposal aimed to benefit all interested parties. Mexico's outstanding external debt would be reduced; it would have sufficient funds to pay the interest on the remaining debt, which would please both the security holders and the International Committee. The oil companies could pay the higher export tax at a discount without reducing their profits. Lastly, Mexico's credit rating would be greatly improved as a by-product of the scheme.[52]

Lamont immediately saw the flaws in this arrangement. American bankers would compromise their integrity with in-

---

[52] Turlington, Mexico and Her Foreign Creditors, 283-284.

vestors if they attempted to purchase bonds at a fraction of the price at which they had originally offered them to the public. Additionally, the Committee had long maintained that the bondholders it represented were entitled to full value for their holdings together with accrued interest. Since the security pledged to cover the interest was now in excess of the current interest due, it would clearly be ill-advised for the bankers to profit by persuading holders to accept a fraction of the potential real value of their securities.[53]

Despite the misgivings expressed to Hughes concerning this new obstacle, Lamont arrived in Mexico City on October 8, 1921, with hopes for fruitful discussions. He was to be greatly disappointed. De la Huerta's steadfast insistence that any settlement of the debt question must be linked with an understanding with the oil men proved to be an insurmountable obstacle. The Minister of Finance argued that the proposal was legitimate since each of the many loan agreements stipulated that the government could purchase its bonds on the open market if it wished. Lamont claimed that this right had been forfeited when Mexico fell into arrears on the interest due. De la Huerta then suggested that his plan was not different in effect from the United States' policy of

---

[53] Draft of Letter from Lamont to W.C. Teagle, Chairman of the Committee of Oil Executives, September 19, 1921, FRUS 1921, II, 500-501.

purchasing outstanding Liberty Bonds at a market price below face value. Lamont pointed out that the United States had never fallen behind in interest payments on those bonds. Lamont soon returned to New York without an understanding being reached.[54]

J.P. Morgan probably reflected well, if somewhat crudely, the feelings within the investment banking community when he cabled Lamont upon his return,

> Your cable giving results [of] your Mexican visit perfectly amazing. I did not think any Government of modern times would so frankly proclaim its complete dishonesty or its abandonment of all decent finance or morals.[I] congratulate you in getting out before they stole your pocketbook or watch...congratulations to you personally on your having succeeded in unmasking the villains.[55]

Early in 1922 the State Department held a meeting with representatives of leading American investment banking firms. Then it issued a statement to the press on March 3, 1922, which expressed a strong interest in all future flotations of foreign bonds in the American market. The press release indicated that the bankers voluntarily agreed to consult with the Department before consummating such transactions. The Department would then express an opinion as to the propriety of the issue, then, hopefully, the bankers would proceed in a manner consistent with their patriotic responsibilities.[56]

---

[54] New York Times, October 29, 1921.

[55] Morgan to Lamont, October 25, 1921, Box 192, Lamont Papers.

[56] Press Release issued by Department of State, March 3, 1922, FRUS 1922, I, 556-558.

There is little doubt that this understanding between the Department and the bankers was aimed primarily at Europe. The Republicans were annoyed at the reluctance of America's former allies to honor their debts to the United States. This proved to be particularly irritating in view of the rush to rearm. There was no inclination in Washington to make new funds available to them.

American industrial expansion in the first two years of the new decade had already produced a significant accumulation of surplus capital. With Europe seemingly eliminated as an area for new investments, bankers looked to Latin America. But unless some hard evidence could be shown to potential investors that their funds were secure in Latin America, this area could not be opened up to new investment activity. It was essential, therefore, that Mexico be a showcase of the bankers' efforts on behalf of investors.[57] With this uppermost in mind, Lamont responded positively to still another overture by Obregón in March 1922.

On June 2, 1922, de la Huerta met in New York with Lamont and representatives of the various foreign sections of the International Committee.[58] After two weeks of hard bar-

---

[57] Kane, "Bankers and Diplomats," 337-338.

[58] In addition to the British, Dutch, Swiss and Belgian representatives, a German observer was present although, German bankers were not yet represented on the Committee.

gaining, an agreement was finally concluded on June 16, 1922, subject to ratification by Obregón and the Mexican Congress. The accord covered all external obligations of the Mexican government held by foreign investors (excluding the Huerta issues), the debt of the government-controlled railways and certain internal obligations held primarily by foreigners.[59]

The agreement called for the resumption of partial interest payment on January 1, 1923, with the amount to be made available increasing annually until 1928, when full service on the debt was to be resumed. Prior to 1928 the difference between the funds available and the interest due would be paid in scrip carrying a three percent interest rate, beginning in 1926 and maturing in 1943. To guarantee the necessary minimum funds required to meet the interest payments due between 1923 and 1927, the Mexican government would turn over to the International Committee all oil export taxes established through 1921 (including any subsequent increases in those taxes), revenues from a ten per-

---

[59] These internal obligations were the three and five percent loans of 1886 and 1894, respectively, and the bonds of the Caja de Prestamos, a mortgage bank created in 1908 by Mexican banks to make loans for irrigation and agricultural development. Its issues were guaranteed by the government. The bank was badly mismanaged and taken over by the government in 1912. Wynne, State Insolvency, 67. It was estimated that there was one billion pesos in Mexican bonds held by foreigners and that accumulated and unpaid interest since 1913 totalled 400 million pesos. FRUS 1922, II, 686.

cent tax on gross railroad receipts, and the total net operating revenues of the railroads. Interest arrears through January 2, 1923, would be paid in full over forty years, beginning January 1, 1928. No interest on arrears was recognized by the accord.[60]

The ratification of the agreement was delayed until September 29, 1922, because of doubts expressed by Obregón regarding the wisdom of some of its provisions. The Mexican President was concerned because the agreement made no mention of a loan to Mexico. De la Huerta was frustrated and offended that his best efforts did not win immediate approval by Obregón. He assured the President that a new loan was "assured." Yet so long as ratification was delayed, it was impossible for serious talks regarding the loan to take place. Finally, after more than three-months delay, Obregón yielded and the agreement was ratified.[61]

Lamont had kept the State Department fully informed on the progress of the discussions with de la Huerta, and there can be no doubt that the agreement had the Department's blessing. Yet, since the accord made no mention of the retroactivity of Article 27 of the Constitution and did

---

[60] For full text of the Lamont-de la Huerta Agreement, see Turlington, Mexico and Her Foreign Creditors, App. VII.

[61] Ibid., 292-298.

not deal with the question of property rights, it alone was not justification for recognition. Without recognition, no new loan would be forthcoming, since Hughes indicated that he was "disposed to discountenance loans to unrecognized governments."[62]

So long as Hughes maintained this rigid stance, both recognition and the necessary loan would not be forthcoming. But in the latter part of 1922 and early 1923 both the oil interests and Lamont, on behalf of the International Committee, campaigned vigorously for a moderation in State Department policy. They argued that it was best to reach an accommodation with Obregón and de la Huerta who were reasonable men and had brought a degree of stability to Mexico. In 1924 a new election might bring a less reasonable administration to power.[63]

---

[62] Hughes to Herbert Hoover, July 24, 1922, FRUS 1922, II, 764-766.

[63] Robert Freeman Smith, The United States and Revolutionary Nationalism in Mexico, 1916-1932 (Chicago, 1972), 215-218. Smith overstates Lamont's role, depicting him as the moving force in the change that took place in the attitude of the State Department. Smith also errs in his portrayal of the International Committee as "an unofficial instrument of U.S. policy," ibid., 204. Secretary Hughes and the State Department during the Harding and Coolidge administrations did not view it as such. See Kane, "Bankers and Diplomats," for a more balanced view of the International Committee's relationship to the State Department.

For these reasons, and because the Republican administration too faced a presidential campaign the following year,[64] Hughes was receptive when, in February 1923, General James A. Ryan, a representative of the oil interests, brought him a message from Obregón that the Mexican president would welcome the resolution of the outstanding questions between the two nations by a joint commission.[65] Hughes accepted the offer and soon after appointed John Barton Payne and Charles Beecher Warren as the American commissioners.

The discussions, begun in Mexico City on May 14, 1923, have come to be known as the Bucareli Conference (named after the street on which they took place). The conference produced two treaties which, while hardly definitive, enabled the United States to grant recognition to Obregón on September 3, 1923, while enabling both nations to save face.[66] Deliberately vague understandings were reached regarding land expropriated for *ejidos* and subsoil rights. The agreements regarding the latter recognized a Mexican Supreme Court's decision that Article 27 of the Constitution did

---

[64]Murray, The Harding Era, 331, claims that the conference was Harding's idea and that he "more than any other person" was responsible for the recognition of Obregón.

[65]Alberto J. Pani, Las Conferencias de Bucareli (Mexico City, 1953), 88-91.

[66]Warren became the new Ambassador to Mexico on March 31, 1924, serving until October 15, 1924.

not apply retroactively to holdings of persons who had performed some "positive act" in regard to their land prior to the promulgation of the Constitution. The definition of "positive act" was so broad as to be meaningless.[67]

It might have been expected that the resolution of these sensitive areas, however imperfectly, and the granting of recognition would have spawned a new era in Mexican-American relations and facilitated a gradual return to fiscal responsibility. This was not to be the case. The oil companies immediately protested the subsoil agreements as being ambiguous and clearly less than they had expected. Dissidents in Mexico desired to embarrass Obregón for political purposes and painted the Bucareli agreements as a humiliating sellout.

When Obregón named Plutarco Calles as his choice to succeed him in the presidency, de la Huerta resigned as Minister and headed the opposition party as its candidate. Alberto Pani, who succeeded de la Huerta as Minister of Finance, precipitated an armed revolt by his proud predecessor, when he made public an estimated budget deficit of approximately 37 million pesos for the first nine months of 1923. It was implied that this deficit was primarily the result of de la Huerta's mismanagement of the department.

---

[67]United States Department of State, *Proceedings of the United States-Mexico Commission Convened at Mexico City, May 14, 1923* (Washington, D.C., 1925).

Although the bitter exchange that followed was largely election year rhetoric,[68] it did contribute to a brief but costly rebellion.

Prior to the outbreak of de la Huerta's revolt, it had appeared likely that the accord would go into effect as scheduled. Before the end of 1923, Mexico had deposited the minimum required 30 million pesos with the Committee.[69] By October 1923 over 50 percent of the outstanding bonds covered by the Lamont-de la Huerta agreement had been deposited by the holders with the Committee as called for in the accord.[70] Six months later 90 percent of the outstanding securities had been deposited.[71] The first interest payment on the bonds deposited was announced on March 28, 1924.[72]

---

[68] See Mexico. Secretaría de Hacienda y Crédito Público. La controversia Pani-de la Huerta: Documentos para la Historia de la última Asonda Militar (Mexico City, 1924).

[69] Turlington, Mexico and Her Foreign Creditors, 299.

[70] Total bonds deposited were in excess of $250 million by the end of September 1923. Ira Parchin to Lamont, September 28, 1923, Box 192, Lamont Papers.

[71] The bonds deposited in accordance with the Lamont-de la Huerta agreement were held by nationals of eight countries in the following approximate percentages: United States, 20%; Britain, 34%; France, 23%; Netherlands, 9%; Switzerland, Belgium, and Germany, 4% each and Mexico, 1%. Morrow to Frank B. Kellogg, November 9, 1928, Morrow Papers.

[72] Turlington, Mexico and Her Foreign Creditors, 299.

The cost of putting down the de la Huerta rebellion, although not significant in itself,[73] was sufficient when combined with other factors to render it impossible for Obregón to honor the agreement with Lamont. The Lamont-de la Huerta accord had been predicated on the assumption that the proceeds from the oil export tax would continue to rise. Unfortunately, 1922 had been a peak year with the duties exceeding 27.6 million pesos as compared with some 12 million pesos in 1921.[74] By 1923 a significant decline in receipts to 18 million pesos signaled the beginning of a dramatic fall in the oil export tax revenues. In 1927 this source of funds had declined to only five million pesos.[75]

The reasons for this turnaround are many. The controversy over Article 27 made many oil companies unwilling to invest further in Mexican oil fields. The oil production and oil export taxes were deemed too high. Competition from new Venezuelan and Colombian oil fields made Mexican production less important. Aggravating the situation still further

---

[73] Pani estimated the total cost of the campaign at 60 million pesos. While this is undoubtedly an overstatement made for political purposes, Mexico could ill-afford even a fraction of that figure. Mexico, Secretaría de Hacienda y Crédito Público. Memoria de la Secretaría de Hacienda y Crédito Público correspondiente a los años fiscales de 1923, 1924, 1925 (Mexico City, 1926), 47.

[74] Wynne, State Insolvency, 73 fn.

[75] Ibid.; Turlington, Mexico and Her Foreign Creditors, 312 fn.

was the fact of higher production costs in Mexico, which resulted from the exhaustion of most coastal wells and the need to develop interior fields with comparatively lower yields.[76]

Obregón attempted to secure a loan from the International Committee secured against the new oil production tax revenues. Since oil production was already declining his request was refused. Unable therefore to honor the terms of the agreement, Obregón suspended the Lamont-de la Huerta agreement on June 30, 1924.

---

[76]*Ibid.*

CHAPTER III

AMBASSADOR JAMES ROCKWELL SHEFFIELD

Harding's death on August 2, 1923, while the Bucareli discussions were under way in Mexico City, had virtually no impact on the direction of American policy toward Mexico since Secretary of State Hughes remained at the helm under Coolidge. It was Hughes who recognized the Obregón government on August 31, 1923, and who recommended Charles Beecher Warren to be Ambassador to Mexico.[1] Coolidge demonstrated only passing interest in Mexican-American relations while serving out the balance of Harding's term.

The suspension of the Lamont-de la Huerta agreement, while disconcerting, was not of itself a harbinger of a deterioration in relations between the two nations. However, certain pronouncements by Plutarco Calles, Obregón's handpicked successor, while campaigning for the presidency in early 1924, aroused anxieties among foreign governments and investors alike. Calles charged that, "the foreign capitalist has not come to Mexico to develop it, but to exploit it, to take every thing, but to give nothing."[2] Later he

---

[1] Warren served as Ambassador from March 31, 1924, until James Rockwell Sheffield presented his credentials on October 15, 1924.

[2] Plutarco Elías Calles' speech, February 26, 1924, in Robert H. Murray, ed. and trans., Mexico Before the World: Public Documents and Addresses of Plutarco Elías Calles (New York, 1927), 93.

modified this stand somewhat by declaring: "Those who desire to invest their money in the development of this [Mexico's] natural wealth should be protected and they are protected under our laws." It was however, "one thing to comply with the laws and another thing to try to evade them and all the more so if these privileges make Mexicans the slaves of capital."[3] Calles' election in June 1924 did little to relieve international anxieties.

In late summer of 1924, Warren resigned as Ambassador and James Rockwell Sheffield was appointed his successor. Sheffield was a prosperous New York attorney and a faithful Republican without any diplomatic experience. Undoubtedly his appointment resulted from his influence in New York state politics and his numerous friendships with Republican stalwarts like Chief Justice William Howard Taft and Elihu Root.

Prior to Sheffield's departure for Mexico, Root offered him sound advice based on years of diplomatic experience. Root wrote that the "great body of intelligent people" in Mexico "have grown sufficiently tired of the chaos of the last few years to make a persistent effort for law and order" and that they were "very desirous to rehabilitate their country." The United States, Root contended, was best able

---

[3] Calles interview in El Democrata, April 18, 1924, quoted in ibid., 39-40.

to help Mexico, and the Mexicans would gratefully accept that help "if it can be given in such a way as to avoid any suspicion of assumed superiority."[4]

Sheffield presented his credentials to the lame duck Obregón government on October 15, 1924, just three weeks before Coolidge was elected in his own right to a full four-year term. Unfortunately, Sheffield approached his first and final diplomatic assignment with less than an open mind. A year after taking his post he wrote to Nicholas Murray Butler, President of Columbia University, that he had "expected to find corruption, ignorance and cruelty" in Mexico and was not "disappointed in my expectations."[5] With these preconceptions Sheffield's tenure in Mexico City was doomed to be an unhappy period for Mexican-American relations.

Ironically, while Washington was sending an ambassador to Mexico who expressed admiration for the unfortunate policies of former Ambassador Henry Lane Wilson,[6] political and economic conditions in Mexico were improving to a degree

---

[4] Elihu Root to James Rockwell Sheffield, August 19, 1924, Box 7, James Rockwell Sheffield Papers, Yale University Library, New Haven, Connecticut (Hereafter cited as Sheffield Papers.)

[5] Sheffield to Nicolas Murray Butler, November 17, 1925, Box 8, ibid.

[6] Sheffield to William Howard Taft, April 22, 1927, Box 8, ibid.

which might have allowed for a real improvement in relations between the two nations. During 1924 rigid economies and tax reforms had reduced the accumulated deficit carryover by approximately one-third.[7] Calles pleased observers by expressing his interest in balancing the budget and returning Mexico to fiscal stability.[8] He demonstrated his firm resolve by instituting programs aimed at strengthening the monetary system and bolstering economic expansion.

In January 1925 Secretary of State Hughes tendered his long-planned resignation, and Frank B. Kellogg, Ambassador to Great Britain, was named his successor. Although Hughes was an experienced and perspicacious statesman, Kellogg's appointment was to augur well for Mexican-American relations. Hughes vigorously defended the interests of American investors and businessmen in Mexico even at the expense of better understanding with that government. Kellogg was less dogmatic, more flexible, sometimes to a fault, in his approach to the longstanding Mexican-American friction. Although his age, temperament, volatile personality and vacillation caused numerous difficult moments during his three year reign, Kellogg was the catalyst for an eventual improved policy toward Mex-

---

[7]Wynne, State Insolvency, 74.

[8]John W.F. Dulles, Yesterday in Mexico (Austin, 1961), 281.

ico.[9] Coolidge gave Kellogg a free hand in the management of the department.

The year 1925 opened on a hopeful note for the International Committee. In January, Calles sent Alberto Pani to New York to confer with Lamont concerning the possibility of a modification of the 1922 accord and a new loan of $60 million. This sum was to be used to liquidate the budget deficit, meet the interest owed under the Lamont- de la Huerta agreement and facilitate the establishment of the new Bank of Mexico. This bank would be the sole institution authorized to issue Mexican currency. Lamont vigorously opposed any modification of the 1922 accord and deemed the loan to be far above Mexico's actual needs. He viewed the proposed bank as less important to Mexico's long-term financial well-being than a clear indication that the government intended to honor the agreements of 1922 in full. He suggested that a loan of $20 million was possible if the interest due in 1924 was paid, the railways were immediately returned to private control and the oil production tax revenues were deposited in New York in accordance with the pro-

---

[9]L. Ethan Ellis, Frank B. Kellogg and American Foreign Relations, 1925-1929 (New Brunswick, N.J., 1961), 7-8; Hugh Wilson, Chief of Current Information under Kellogg, vividly portrays his volatile personality in Diplomat Between Wars (New York, 1941), 174-177.

visions of the 1922 accord.[10]

Discussions in New York and in Mexico City brought the Committee and the Mexican government to the brink of an agreement for the resumption of service on the foreign debt and a new loan. By August 1925 Pani reported to the Committee that further economies had rendered the previously desired $60 million loan excessive. This statement was accompanied by an announcement that Calles still deemed the Bank of Mexico essential to Mexico's financial reconstruction and that it would be inaugurated on August 31, 1925.[11]

Lamont responded in no uncertain terms that such action on the part of the Calles government would constitute an irrevocable violation of the 1922 accord. Funds which should be applied to the service of the foreign debt under provisions of the Lamont-de la Huerta agreement would be diverted to the bank.[12] The Committee would be compelled to declare Mexico in default and release the bondholders from the agreement. He hinted that the bondholders might then pressure their respective governments to take action

---

[10] Mexico. Secretaría de Hacienda y Crédito Público. La deuda exterior de Mexico (Mexico City, 1926), 169-174.

[11] Turlington, Mexico and Her Foreign Creditors, 305; Dulles, Yesterday in Mexico, 283.

[12] In 1925 the Mexican government contributed approximately 55.7 million pesos to the Bank of Mexico in exchange for most of the bank's shares. Ibid.

to protect their interest.[13]

Meanwhile, Ambassador Sheffield had quickly discovered the situation in Mexico to be precisely as he had feared it was. Calles was a proud man who had no inclination to please the American representative, who hid his deep feelings of superiority so thinly. Moreover, Sheffield made it evident that he intended to represent American business interests first and to work to reduce tensions only secondarily. Sheffield failed to heed Root's admonition that "whatever you want them [Mexicans] to do find some way for them to do it which will not infringe upon their personal dignity."[14] Sheffield quickly lost patience with Mexican recalcitrance and soon was sending off reports to the State Department and to personal friends detailing Mexican stubbornness, their alleged bolshevistic tendencies and how he was becoming frustrated. He wrote to William Phelps, a Yale professor, that "I have an almost impossible task here. I do not expect to succeed--that is the tragedy of my coming."[15]

Sheffield's attitude toward Mexico transcended what for others might merely have been conflicting political ideologies or an inability to appreciate a distinctively different culture. Sheffield's response was primarily emotional,

---

[13]Turlington, Mexico and Her Foreign Creditors, 306.

[14]Root to Sheffield, October 1, 1924, Box 7, Sheffield Papers.

[15]Sheffield to William Phelps, November 12, 1925, Box 8, ibid.

emanating from a racist hatred of non-Anglo-Saxons, an almost paranoiac fear of "bolshevics," and runaway patriotism. He wrote to Butler that the Mexican government was "shot through with bolshevism" but that the leaders were primarily motivated by "greed, a wholly Mexican view of nationalism and an Indian, not Latin, hatred of all peoples not on the reservation." He further pointed out that there was "very little white blood in the Cabinet," and he went on to offer a highly inaccurate breakdown of the racial composition of that body.[16]

Later, when Kellogg ceased to listen to his inflamatory advice, Sheffield wrote Republican Senator James W. Wadsworth Jr. of New York, that American policy was "an encouragement to the bolshevist practices of the present Mexican Government."[17]

Sheffield's patriotism was easily offended as was his personal dignity. Both were undoubtedly made more sensitive by his blatant racism. He confided to Butler that it was "an unpleasant duty to try and maintain relations between the two countries when every friendly overture must come from me and all the hostility open or veiled from them. It does not comport with my Americanism to have the United

---

[16] Sheffield to Butler, November 17, 1925, Box 8, ibid.
[17] Sheffield to James W. Wadsworth Jr., June 3, 1926, Box 8, ibid.

States make all the advances and do all the overlooking and all the forgiving."[18] Later he boasted to Wadsworth that he "tried to be a red-blooded American south of the Rio Grande."[19]

In addition to his emotional distaste for the Mexicans, Sheffield undoubtedly was motivated by his intimacy with the American business establishment, his conservatism, and his view of the role of ambassador as primarily a protector of American investments in Mexico. James T. Williams, a Hearst reporter who traveled extensively in Mexico while Sheffield was ambassador and had numerous frank discussions with him, recorded that Sheffield had "gone to Mexico with the determination to make the Mexicans pay their claims and stop their nonsense."[20] American firms interested in Mexico were abundantly aware of Sheffield's inclinations. Harold Walker, who represented the Edward L. Doheny oil interests, wrote Sheffield upon his resignation that, "from the time you took your post in Mexico, all American oil companies, particularly our own, have felt deep confidence in the protection of their properties. It is not an over-

---

[18] Sheffield to Butler, November 17, 1925, Box 8, ibid.

[19] Sheffield to Wadsworth, March 4, 1926, Box 8, ibid.

[20] James T. Williams, "The Reminiscences of James T. Williams" (2 vols., Oral History Research Office, Columbia University, New York, 1961), II, 562.

statement to say that up to now we believe you have saved our properties."[21]

Throughout his stay in Mexico, Sheffield was a consistent advocate of firmness with the Mexican government and repeatedly called for the protection of American property whatever the consequences. When Calles, early in 1925, expressed his unhappiness with the commitments made by Obregon in the Bucareli agreements, Kellogg consulted Sheffield as to how the Department might best handle Mexico's second thoughts. Sheffield assured the Secretary that it was imperative that the United States refuse to compromise its principles.[22]

A reflection of Sheffield's early influence on Kellogg was an unfortunate statement written by Kellogg and Sheffield and released to the press on June 12, 1925. The statement reflected well Sheffield's call for "firmness." It stated that the government of the United States would continue to support the Mexican government "only so long as it protects American lives and American rights and complies with its international engagements and obligations. The Government of Mexico is now on trial before the world."[23]

---

[21]Harold Walker to Sheffield, July 11, 1927, Box 8, Sheffield Papers.

[22]Ellis, <u>Frank B. Kellogg</u>, 27.

[23]Kellogg to H.F. Arthur Schoenfeld, June 12, 1925, FRUS 1925, II, 517-518.

While Sheffield pursued his "hard line" policy in Mexico City, Lamont displayed a more "enlightened" approach in New York. By October 1925, he had concluded that "friendliness counts with these people [Mexicans] more than I can say." Apparently he had subscribed to a philosophy implicit in a comment made to him by a Mexican that "you can lead us around with a lump of sugar but you cannot drive us an inch."[24]

From International Committee sources in Mexico, Lamont had learned that the law under which the Bank of Mexico was being operated was in accordance with sound banking practice and that the managers of the bank were "careful people." This apparently overcame the displeasure Lamont had voiced at the founding of the institution. He expressed his hope to Benjamin Strong of the New York Federal Reserve Bank that "some sort of relationship" could be established between the Federal Reserve Bank of New York and the Mexican bank which would be advantageous to both nations.[25]

With this obstacle effectively removed, Lamont again welcomed discussions with Pani concerning the modification of the suspended 1922 accord. A modification of the Lamont-de la Huerta agreement, known as the Lamont-Pani agreement,

---

[24] Lamont to Benjamin Strong, October 23, 1925, Box 192, Lamont Papers.

[25] Ibid.

was quickly concluded and signed on October 23, 1925. The revised agreement provided that funds which the government had failed to deposit with the Committee in 1924 and 1925, as required by the earlier accord, would be deferred and liquidated over an eight year period, beginning on January 1, 1928, with interest at three percent per annum.

The accord also contained several other provisions. The national railways would be returned to private management on December 31, 1925, under conditions which would enable them, through efficient management, to earn and pay the full fixed charges on their outstanding bonds. The Mexican government would no longer be directly responsible for the railway debt except to the extent it was bound by previous guarantees. The oil export taxes would now be applicable only to the direct debt. In addition to these tax revenues the Committee was to receive $5 million U.S. gold annually from the oil production tax receipts up to a fixed maximum payment for both taxes together.[26]

Unfortunately this agreement did not alleviate tensions between the two nations. On December 18, 1925, a new petroleum law was enacted. It aimed at implementing Article 27 of the Constitution. The law declared that the ownership of all petroleum deposits was vested in the nation. For-

---

[26] For full text see, "Statement of Modification of Plan and Agreement dated June 16, 1922," Box 192, ibid., or Turlington, Mexico and Her Foreign Creditors, app. ix.

eigners, who had begun exploitation of their land prior to May 1, 1917, could obtain "confirmatory concessions" from the government through December 31, 1926, on the condition that they formally agree to be considered Mexicans and therefore relinquish recourse to the protection of their governments in respect to these concessions. Americans found this provision to be particularly offensive. The concessions were to be valid for not more than 50 years. Thus even rights acquired prior to the promulgation of the 1917 Constitution must be confirmed.[27]

Foreign oil operators refused to comply with the conditions of the law. They were then denied drilling permits by the governments and were informed that they had forfeited all previous rights. As a result producers of approximately 50 to 70 percent of Mexico's oil yield were forced to halt operations.[28]

Almost simultaneous with the petroleum law, an Alien Land Law was enacted on December 23, 1925. It prohibited foreigners from owning land within 100 kilometers of Mexico's borders and 50 kilometers of the coast. Additionally,

---

[27] Ibid., 309; Dulles, Yesterday in Mexico, 319.

[28] The Mexican government claimed the figure was 50 percent, but Guy Stevens of the Association of Producers of Petroleum maintained that 70 percent was more accurate. J. Fred Rippy, Jose Vasconcelos and Guy Stevens, American Policies Abroad: Mexico (Chicago, 1928), 210-211.

aliens and foreign companies were excluded from ownership of more than a minority interest in agricultural development lands. As with the petroleum law, the land law required that foreigners who exploited Mexico's natural resources must forfeit their right to protection from their governments. The question of retroactivity also arose, and it too was much contested. In the United States and Europe the law was denounced as confiscatory.

Both laws violated the spirit, if not the letter, of the Bucareli agreements. Calles maintained that he was not bound by these accords. A heated exchange followed between the Mexican government and the State Department. Sheffield steadfastly advocated firmness. Kellogg vacillated between mild reproach and vehement protest.[29] Others, particularly the Hearst press, Senator Albert B. Fall, the National Association for the Protection of American Rights in Mexico led by Edward L. Doheny, and the Association of Producers of Petroleum called for armed intervention. Only the revelation of Fall and Doheny's participation in the growing Teapot Dome scandal cooled the public outcry for intervention.[30]

The Mexican government insisted that it must have control of its own natural resources. It maintained this stance

---

[29] Ellis, *Frank B. Kellogg*, 29-33.

[30] Dulles, *Yesterday in Mexico*, 322-323.

in the face of drastically declining revenues from the vital oil production and export taxes. The State Department, although it was under constant pressure from the oil industry which was faced with the January 1, 1927, deadline for obtaining the "confirmatory concessions," never seriously considered armed intervention. Sheffield complained to Butler that "public opinion in the United States is so indifferent to what is going on South of the Rio Grande and so ignorant of the state of affairs that any attempt at firmness is apt to be looked upon either as a sign of imperialism or a threat of military intervention and war."[31]

Throughout 1926 Sheffield tried to persuade Kellogg to take a hard line toward Mexico, but to no avail. Kellogg had come under the influence of Robert E. Olds, the Secretary's former law partner and an Assistant Secretary of State since September 1, 1925. Soon after joining the Department, Olds involved himself "heavily" in Mexican policy making. Kellogg came to rely on Olds and gave the Assistant Secretary broad leeway in the formulation of Mexican policy. It was Olds who, with the apparent blessing of Kellogg, slowly moved the State Department away from the kinds of policy being advocated by Sheffield and

---

[31] Sheffield to Butler, November 17, 1925, Box 8, Sheffield Papers.

towards a more "enlightened" approach to Mexican-American relations. This is not to say that Olds consciously took over the formulation of Mexican policy with the intention of bringing about the changes which eventually occurred, but rather that he was a man of "first rate" talents who brought an open mind to a problem that had too long been handled in old ways by conservative career diplomats inhibited by unhappy precedent. Olds acted decisively where others vacillated. He attempted new approaches while others merely reacted. He took a long range view of Mexican-American relations while others were myopic.[32]

Olds was a realist who refused to defend the Department's past unsuccessful policies toward Mexico. He wrote candidly to Dwight Morrow at the time of the latter's appointment as Ambassador to Mexico in 1927, saying:

> Our officials who handle these Mexican matters are always subject to the temptation to indulge a cynical pessimism, and give way to impatient and emotional reaction. At certain junctures years ago they have done so with unfortunate results which plague and embarrass us today. If anything is plain from our experience with Mexico it is the fact that an ideal solution for all concerned is not to be expected. We have never attained any such goal, and it is not likely that we shall. We have got to do the best we can within the limits which we ourselves fix.[33]

This extremely pragmatic approach to the Mexican problem

---

[32]Ellis, Frank B. Kellogg, 17, 24-25.

[33]Memorandum from Robert E. Olds to Dwight W. Morrow, dated July 22, 1927, Morrow Papers.

contrasted sharply with Sheffield's attitude, but it would hold Olds in good stead throughout his tenure in the Department.[34]

Throughout 1926 Olds and former ambassador Charles Beecher Warren counseled Kellogg to avoid a too rigid stance against Mexico. Because of his first-hand knowledge of Mexico and its leaders, Warren, much to Sheffield's displeasure, was frequently consulted by Kellogg. Several notes sent by the Department to Calles in 1926 were written by Olds and/or Warren. These reflected the moderate views of these two men.[35] The notes contained no threats but rather attempted to convince Calles to issue a series of regulatory decrees, as he had hinted, aimed at modifying the objectionable laws and protecting American oil and land interests.

Throughout his tenure in Mexico Sheffield was to be a major obstacle to the implementation of State Department policy. Sheffield held steadfastly to his contention that the United States had an obligation to its nationals not to concede the validity, in whole or in part, of the Mexican legislation. To Senator Wadsworth of the Foreign Relations Committee, Sheffield pleaded that "the billion and a half

---

[34]Olds was Assistant Secretary of State until June 30, 1927, when he was made Undersecretary, a position he held until June 30, 1928. After his departure for private law practice he continued to perform certain services for the Department.

[35]Sheffield to Taft, January 22, 1927 and Sheffield to Wadsworth, April 7, 1926, Box 8, Sheffield Papers.

American dollars invested in Mexico as well as the lives of our nationals are at stake." All American investments, he argued, were "entitled to protection in the fullest extent of the power of our government." Sheffield further held that, "Any failure to be firm would be disastrous."[36]

Sheffield felt that because of his familiarity with Mexico and its leaders he was best suited to formulate Mexican policy. He hinted at offering his resignation if his policy of "absolute protection to American interests" was not accepted as the "firm policy of the Administration." In an apparent attempt to elevate his argument to a higher plain, Sheffield contended that "the United States with its power and its wealth and its well orderly [sic] civilization owes to Mexico as well as to itself from a moral point of view all the help it can render to uplift and set on its feet this backward people."[37]

While in Mexico Sheffield was in regular, sometimes daily, contact with Chandler P. Anderson, who for more than a decade had been a lobbiest for the oil interests. Anderson and Sheffield shared common goals and worked harmoniously in the pursuit of their ends. Sheffield candidly informed Anderson of his conflicts with the State Department and the frustrations he experienced. Anderson frequently

---

[36]Sheffield to Wadsworth, March 4, 1926, Box 8, ibid.
[37]Ibid.

visited with Department officials and sounded out Kellogg as to his attitude toward Mexican problems. It was Anderson who informed Sheffield that Kellogg was "not willing to go the full length of the policy which you had recommended."[38] This was a gross understatement.

Early in 1926 Sheffield had drafted an ultimatum and had asked Kellogg to send it to the Mexican government. The note reflected Sheffield's "brinkmanship." His philosophy at the time was that, "all we've got to do is threaten them. Call their bluff."[39] Kellogg had informed the ambassador that the United States would not threaten a foreign government unless it intended to back up that threat.[40] Sheffield's reactionary stance caused him to be systematically excluded from the State Department decision-making process. Thus he was left almost totally in the dark regarding policy toward Mexico, sometimes for as long as months at a time. Now abundantly aware of Sheffield's position, Kellogg and Olds attempted to isolate him, hoping he would resign.

Sheffield became angry when Kellogg ignored his policy

---

[38]Chandler P. Anderson to Sheffield, March 30, 1926, Box 8, ibid.

[39]Sheffield to Kellogg, January 12, 1926, Box 8, ibid.

[40]Williams, "Reminiscences," II, 562-563.

recommendations and apparently did not make them known to Coolidge. He wrote Anderson that whether or not Kellogg approved of his recommendations, the Secretary was "under an official obligation to let the man who controls foreign relations" at least read his memorandum. Sheffield considered appealing directly to the President since he believed he had the right to know "what the attitude of the Administration is toward the Mexican situation." The Ambassador was "confident that the President can not have been kept fully informed," convinced that this was "the kind of blunder that amounts to a crime."[41]

When, in April 1926, it appeared possible that the State Department would accept proposed Mexican regulations which would amend the petroleum law, Sheffield again complained to Anderson that it was a "distinct compromise of principle and in the long run fatal to achieving positive results in dealing with Mexico under her extremely socialist Constitution."[42] Sheffield was bitter at having been passed over in the formulation of the American responses to events in Mexico. He revealed to Wadsworth that he "was not consulted in any way as to the last two notes and was not informed of the position the Department took in the

---

[41] Sheffield to Chandler Anderson, March 30, 1926, Box 8, Sheffield Papers.

[42] Sheffield to Chandler Anderson, April 7, 1926, Box 8, ibid.

last note until six days after a copy had been handed to Ambassador Tellez." Sheffield claimed that it put him at a "considerable disadvantage" in dealing with the Mexican government.[43]

There can be little question that Sheffield's dealings with the Mexican government were far from desirable. Still, this condition had its genesis more in the reactions of the Mexican leaders to Sheffield's arrogance than in the disinclination of Department policymakers to share their decisions with him. By 1926 Sheffield had so antagonized Calles that the Mexican president would not see him.[44] Undoubtedly Sheffield's inability to get along with Calles had its origins in his belief that Calles' "real views differ but little from those held by the Soviet regime in Russia," and that "his actions indicate sympathy with Bolshevism."[45] As the self-appointed protector of American capitalists, Sheffield could hardly communicate with the Mexican with an open mind.

By spring 1926 Sheffield was abundantly aware that his advocacy of firmness with Mexico was viewed in many quarters as narrow and dangerous. He therefore attempted to place his stance in a broader, hopefully more palatable, perspective.

---

[43] Sheffield to Wadsworth, April 7, 1926, Box 8, ibid.

[44] Williams, "Reminiscences," II, 562.

[45] Sheffield to Julian S. Mason, October 21, 1927, Box 9, Sheffield Papers.

He wrote to Henry W. Anderson, American representative to the claims commission, that the protection of American property throughout Latin America depended on the protection of American property in Mexico. "Weakness here [Mexico] will be assumed to be the national policy and taken advantage of elsewhere." He warned that while "firmness will not necessarily lead to serious consequences," as Kellogg seemed to believe, "lack of it certainly will."[46]

For the balance of his tenure in Mexico Sheffield clothed his call for firm actin in the guise of a broad Latin American policy. He cautioned Wadsworth that "if we are going to protect our ever increasing investments in Latin America, it will only be brought about by a firm and unyielding policy toward Mexico."[47] To Chandler Anderson he confided, in a back-handed swipe at Kellogg, that what was needed was "a strong man in the State Department who would reorganize the Latin American and Mexican divisions...and establish a continuing policy that would bring results."[48]

Sheffield frequently expressed fear that the longer the State Department delayed in adopting the kinds of policies he advocated the less likely that it would bring the desired results. He particularly bemoaned the fact that Calles "was less securely established in power" earlier and

---

[46]Sheffield to Henry W. Anderson, April 7, 1926, Box 8, ibid.

[47]Sheffield to Wadsworth, April 7, 1926, Box 8, ibid.

[48]Sheffield to C. Anderson, June 1, 1926, Box 8, ibid.

"firmness on our part would have compelled him to yield lest he lose his job and perhaps, his life."[49]

Frequently, in the summer of 1926, it appeared that Sheffield had despaired of achieving any kind of satisfactory change in the Department's policy. He confided to Anderson his disappointment at having his suggestions and advice "totally" disregarded in Washington, "to the serious detriment and even total ruin of our nationals and to the annihilation of the influence of the United States in controlling this radical Mexican Government."[50] A few days later he wondered in a letter to Wadsworth, "just how long our Government will pursue its present policy of neglect of American rights under international law." The Ambassador voiced his belief that the current policy encouraged the "bolshevist practices" of the Calles government.[51]

In contrast to Sheffield's blatant pessimism, Lamont viewed conditions in Mexico more optimistically. In June 1926 he expressed the opinion that conditions were improving and also satisfaction that the Mexican government was making regular payments in accordance with the Lamont-Pani accord. Yet, experience led him to caution a group considering the construction of a new Mexican highway system that

---

[49] Ibid.

[50] Ibid.

[51] Sheffield to Wadsworth, June 3, 1926, Box 8, ibid.

the time had not yet arrived when Mexico could borrow new funds on the world's money markets.[52]

H.F. Arthur Schoenfeld was Counselor to the Embassy at Mexico City and a staunch supporter of Sheffield's policies. While Schoenfeld was on leave in the United States, Sheffield asked him to sound out the Department policymakers as to the current policy toward Mexico. Schoenfeld consulted with Olds and Joseph Grew, Undersecretary of State, and they informed him that, in their view, American public opinion would not support "strong policies" in Mexico. They also felt that the protection of property rights would be an unacceptable excuse for a harder line.[53]

In July 1926, in still another attempt to influence policy, Sheffield sent a lengthy statement of his views to Kellogg. Sheffield ignored Schoenfeld's report on the Department's evaluation of current public opinion and emphasized the protection of property rights under international law. He unabashedly argued that it was the "duty" of the United States to use force to protect the rights and property of American citizens. If "forceful representations" did not bring about the desired results, he asked Kellogg, would "self respect," and "national safety and honor" not require intervention?[54]

---

[52] Lamont to Frank G. McLoughlin, June 21, 1926, Box 192, Lamont Papers.

[53] Schoenfeld to Sheffield, June 28, 1926, Box 8, Sheffield Papers.

[54] Sheffield to Kellogg, July 1, 1926, Box 8, ibid.

Again appealing to a racism he apparently felt Kellogg shared, Sheffield reminded the Secretary that they were "dealing with Latin Indians" who "recognize no argument but force." He further argued that "fairness and justice" were sentiments lacking in Mexicans and any appeal to those virtues must result in failure. The American people would support armed intervention in Mexico if the facts were revealed to them.[55] The latter was to be a recurring theme in Sheffield's correspondence.

Sheffield made no fine distinctions between the leaders of the Calles government and the bandits who had plagued Mexico since the 1911 revolution. He claimed that the only difference between revolutionaries and bandits was "the difference between success and failure."[56] This insensitivity to the role of former revolutionaries in Mexican politics in part explains Sheffield's failure as ambassador.

It is perhaps ironic that although Sheffield's position was rejected as the bases of American policy, that the United States, in the latter part of 1926 and early 1927, should be moving in the direction so frequently espoused by the Ambassador. In August 1926 Sheffield returned to the United States on a leave that lasted until late November. Together with Chandler Anderson he continued to urge the Department to take

---

[55] Ibid.
[56] Ibid.

firm action against Mexico. Were it not for new developments in Mexico and in Nicaragua Sheffield's efforts would undoubtedly have been to no avail.

The 1917 Mexican constitution had contained several provisions aimed at restricting the Catholic Church which had been an ally of the Díaz regime and was much despised by the revolutionaries. For the most part these provisions had been unenforced prior to 1926. Calles issued a presidential decree in July 1926 which ordered the enforcement of Article 130 of the constitution. These provisions required that "ministers of religious creeds" be considered as persons "exercising a profession" and subject to all laws enacted regulating that profession. It was further provided that the number of such "ministers" needed in a locality should be determined exclusively by the state legislatures. Only native born Mexicans could be ministers. Clerics could not "criticize the fundamental laws of the country, the authorities in particular or the government in general." They could neither vote, hold office, nor assemble for political purposes.[57]

The hierarchy of the Catholic Church in Mexico responded to the decree by charging the government with persecution. As a symbolic act of protest all public worship conducted

---

[57]Turlington, Mexico and Her Foreign Creditors, 311 fn.

by priests was suspended indefinitely. Important Catholic leaders called upon their fellow Catholics to demonstrate their displeasure through an economic boycott of all goods not absolutely necessary. The hope was that the faltering economy could not withstand this additional pressure and that the government would be compelled to abrogate the offensive decree to save itself.

In the United States this drastic anticlerical policy aroused the anger of powerful Catholic pressure groups, which vigorously protested to the State Department. Although all the Department could do in this purely domestic matter was express its concern and take unofficial action to resolve the friction between the Mexican government and the Church, the pressure emanating from these highly vocal groups undoubtedly contributed to the Department's inclination to take a firmer stand on other issues.[58]

The second event which influenced American policymakers was the involvement of Mexico in Nicaragua's domestic turmoil.[59] The United States had taken an active interest in that Central American nation since 1909, when the Taft ad-

---

[58] The impact of Mexico's religious struggle on Mexican-American relations is detailed in Elizabeth Ann Rice, The Diplomatic Relations between the United States and Mexico, as Affected by the Struggle for Religious Liberty in Mexico: 1925-1929 (Washington, D.C., 1959).

[59] See Ellis, Frank B. Kellogg, 58-85, for a detailed analysis of the Nicaragua episode and Mexican involvement in it.

ministration gave moral support to a revolution against dictator José Zelaya. The new ruler, Adolfo Díaz, was agreeable to the kind of financial arrangement Theodore Roosevelt had brought about in the Dominican Republic, where the United States took charge of customs collections and administrating the proceeds.

But the Senate balked. An insurrection followed when the Nicaraguan treasury was exhausted. Díaz requested that American marines be landed to restore order. Two thousand marines were dispatched and quickly restored peace. A contingent of 100 marines remained behind as a "legation guard," when the bulk of the force was withdrawn. Despite its size, this force functioned as an agent of stability as long as it remained in Nicaragua.

In 1923 the Central American states concluded a treaty by which they agreed not to recognize governments coming to power through revolution. The United States supported this accord and Coolidge announced that in anticipation of the stability which would result from this agreement, the balance of the marines would be withdrawn from Nicaragua after the next presidential inauguration. Thus when Carlos Solórzano defeated Emiliano Chamorro, the marines departed on August 4, 1925. Unfortunately, Chamorro claimed that the election was a fraud and through quasi-constitutional means made himself president. The United States refused to recognize the usurper. Chaos followed and Díaz again emerged as President and was so recognized by the United States.

But liberal Juan Sacasa, who had been elected vice-president with Solórzano and had fled into exile, landed on the Carribean coast with an invasion force. Supported by Mexico, Sacasa's forces achieved a series of victories against Díaz' army so that by late 1926 they threatened the capital and embarrassed the United States. Mexico provided Sacasa with arms and munitions in hopes that in victory he would support Mexico as a counter-influence against the United States in Latin America.

Once again Chandler Anderson represented important American interests having holdings in Nicaragua. Anderson was a staunch opponent of the leftist Sacasa movement and a firm supporter of the conservative Díaz. He believed that Sacasa was a threat, that he would help spread bolshevik policies he feared were prevalent in Mexico to Nicaragua and eventually throughout Latin America. With the support of Sheffield and Schoenfeld, Anderson argued for armed intervention in Nicaragua to protect American property. He was hopeful, of course, that the use of force in Nicaragua would ease the way for armed intervention in Mexico.[60]

Much to the satisfaction of Anderson and Sheffield,

---

[60] Smith, The United States and Revolutionary Nationalism, 235-239.

Coolidge felt obliged to land marines in Managua, Nicaragua, on January 6, 1927, ostensibly to protect canal rights. This maneuver prevented the fall of the capital. Coolidge then dispatched Henry L. Stimson to Nicaragua as his special envoy in an attempt to bring about a settlement of the civil strife.

Sheffield viewed Coolidge's action as a sign that the United States had finally come to its senses. He wrote Taft: "Those marines in Nicaragua are better than all the diplomatic notes that could be written to the Mexican Government." Mexico, he said, was "one of the countries where the gun is mightier than the pen."[61]

With the assistance of Anderson, Schoenfeld, and representatives of the Catholic Church, Sheffield vigorously pressed his campaign for greater forcefulness in Mexico to protect American rights and property. In a classic example of Sheffield's philosophy, he wrote Schoenfeld: "Property rights are human rights. Oil companies are merely an aggregation of many human beings owning stock."[62] Schoenfeld, who was also encouraged by Coolidge's decision to use force in Nicaragua, assured Sheffield that there was still hope that Coolidge would "face the issue" in Mexico and take action there which would enable the Ambassador to postpone his

---

[61] Sheffield to Taft, March 5, 1927, Box 8, Sheffield Papers.

[62] Sheffield to Schoenfeld, February 1, 1927, Box 8, ibid.

threatened resignation.[63]

Widespread opposition arose in Congress, the press and among certain interest groups to the return of the marines to Nicaragua and to talk of armed intervention in Mexico. Ardent isolationists like William Borah, Robert LaFollette, George Norris and Burton Wheeler attacked intervention in Congress, accusing Coolidge of a return to dollar diplomacy. These men openly ridiculed Kellogg's contention that there was some kind of unholy conspiracy among Nicaraguan, Mexican and Soviet leaders.

The controversy surrounding the possibility of American use of force in Mexico aroused anxieties below the border. Mexican Finance Minister Pani, then in New York to discuss Mexico's financial woes which were threatening the Lamont-Pani accord, voiced his concern repeatedly that the United States was "seeking a ground for intervention."[64]

There can be little doubt that the United States never seriously considered armed intervention in Mexico during the Coolidge administration. Lamont probably accurately summed up the position of the American government when he wrote Augustin Legorreta, head of the Banco Nacional de Mexico. "Nothing is more opposed to his [Coolidge's] thought than any idea of intervention or interference in Mexico's

---

[63]Schoenfeld to Sheffield, February 8, 1927, Box 8, ibid.

[64]Memorandum of Meeting between Morrow, Thomas Cochran and Alberto Pani, February 21, 1927, Morrow Papers.

affairs," Lamont suggested, one week after the marines had landed in Nicaragua. Coolidge and his advisers, Lamont contended, were "animated with the liveliest sense of goodwill toward Mexico."[65]

Lamont was concerned nevertheless. Declining revenues from the oil production and export taxes jeopardized the agreement he had concluded with Pani. Total revenues from the two sources had declined from 55 million pesos in 1924 to 42 million in 1925 and down to 35 million pesos in 1926. It was anticipated that 1927 would bring an even more dramatic decline because of the refusal of the oil companies to conform to the petroleum law's requirements.[66]

The Mexican treasury was in such desperate straits that by early February 1927 Sheffield told Schoenfeld and Anderson that the Lamont-Pani agreement was dead.[67] Lamont was more optimistic. Pani had completed the 1926 payments to the Committee with great difficulty and despite heavy political opposition. The Mexican Finance Minister was highly regarded by Lamont who referred to him as "the conservative influence in the Calles Cabinet."[68] Lamont anticipated that Pani's

___

[65]Lamont to Augustin Legoretta, January 14, 1927, Box 192, Lamont Papers.

[66]Turlington, Mexico and Her Foreign Creditors, 312 fn.

[67]Sheffield to Schoenfeld, February 7, 1927 and Sheffield to Chandler Anderson, February 11, 1927, Box 8, Sheffield Papers.

[68]Lamont to Morrow, January 17, 1927, Box 192, Lamont Papers.

friendship with Obregon, who he assumed would succeed Calles as president, would enable him to choose his post in the new cabinet and would bode well for the bondholders.[69]

As the weeks passed and the United States seemed no closer to adopting his policy on Mexico than it had been prior to the Nicaraguan intervention, Sheffield again despaired. He complained to Anderson that the United States had "lost the opportunity." It had had the Mexican government "in the deepest sort of hole," but alas, the State Department "has permitted them to crawl out." In characteristic self-pity, Sheffield lamented his lot of having "to struggle with two governments--the one you are accredited to and the one back home." It is, he said, "a nerve-destroying job."[70]

Sheffield's attitude toward Mexico was reciprocated by the Mexicans. Mexican Ambassador Manuel C. Tellez confided to Lamont that on several occasions Calles had almost asked for Sheffield's recall since neither he nor his cabinet had confidence in him. Tellez accurately characterized Sheffield as petty, cynical and contemptuous of the Calles administration.[71]

___

[69] Lamont to John Ridgely Carter, March 7, 1927, Box 192, ibid.

[70] Sheffield to Anderson, March 31, 1927, Box 8, Sheffield Papers.

[71] Memorandum of meeting between Tellez and Lamont, March 31, 1927, Morrow Papers.

Sheffield had clearly outlived what little usefulness he might have had. Yet from Mexico City a steady stream of correspondence attacking both the Mexican government and the State Department continued to flow. Sheffield decried the opportunities he alleged the United States had missed for attaining "definite results." He claimed that American policy had a "most disastrous effect" on Mexico in that it was "slowly drifting into revolution and financial and economic chaos."[72]

At the same time that Sheffield was alienating the Mexican authorities, conspiring with Anderson to influence State Department policy to protect private interests in Mexico and regularly criticizing both governments in his private correspondence, he self-righteously swore that as long as he remained in Mexico, he would "loyally" carry out whatever policy was arrived at in Washington, "even though it does not meet with my approval."[73]

It became increasingly evident to Sheffield that the hopes he had entertained early in 1927 that his policies would be adopted by the Department were unfounded. Coolidge refused to use force in Mexico and adopted a policy sometimes referred to as "vigilant patience." Kellogg, still under the influence of Olds, returned to his former more

---

[72] Sheffield to Taft, April 22, 1927 and Sheffield to Chandler Anderson, April 22, 1927, Box 8, Sheffield Papers.

[73] Ibid.

discreet approach. The more vocal members of Congress, the majority of the nation's newspapers, and public opinion in the United States all dictated that no new interventions in Latin America be considered. Since it was unlikely that there would be any significant State Department policy change in the direction he desired, Sheffield left Mexico for the United States, and formally tendered his resignation on July 8, 1927.

CHAPTER IV

AMBASSADOR DWIGHT W. MORROW

Sheffield's resignation as Ambassador undoubtedly was greeted with a sigh of relief in Mexico City. No official of the Calles' administration had ever expressed anything but dismay at Sheffield's approach to Mexican-American relations. None mourned his departure. Yet there was no optimism south of the border regarding the possibility of any significant improvement in relations between the two neighbors. Experience preempted hope.

In Washington disenchantment with Sheffield had been longstanding. Several months before his actual resignation, thought had been given to a possible successor. Dwight Whitney Morrow was recommended to President Coolidge for the post by several individuals including Kellogg and Olds.[1] It is not likely that Coolidge needed to have Morrow's name called to his attention. He and Morrow had been classmates at Amherst College, knew each other quite well and shared a mutual respect. Morrow had been voted by his classmates as the "one most likely to succeed." He had cast his vote for young Calvin Coolidge. Prior to 1927, Coolidge had seriously considered Morrow for several important posts. Only Morrow's partnership in the firm of J.P. Morgan & Company

---

[1]Ellis, <u>Frank B. Kellogg</u>, 48.

caused Coolidge to hesitate in offering him a government position earlier.[2]

Morrow had joined the Morgan firm as a partner early in 1914, after a brief and successful career in corporate law. His dynamism, industriousness and genuine affability had held him in good stead. He quickly rose to an important position in the nation's most influential investment banking firm. Like several other Morgan partners, Morrow devoted considerable time during the war to public service. Beginning in February 1918, he had served in London and Paris as an adviser to the Allied Maritime Transportation Council, which had been formed in 1917 to coordinate Allied shipping policies to counter the German submarine menace. Although Morrow worked only ten months in this capacity, he gained valuable diplomatic experience. While in London he won the friendship and respect of Commander Lewis B. McBride, the assistant naval attaché, who was assigned to the Transportation Council, and George Rublee, an assistant American

---

[2] In mid-1924, when Kellogg was appointed Secretary of State, he recommended Morrow to be his Undersecretary, replacing Joseph Grew, or that he be made an Assistant Secretary, but Coolidge feared public reaction to the naming of a banker. Ibid., 10; Joseph C. Grew, Turbulent Era: A Diplomatic Record of Forty Years, 1904-1941 (2 vols., Boston, 1952), II, 651-653. In November 1925, it was rumored that Coolidge had considered and rejected Morrow as a potential replacement for Secretary of Treasury Andrew Mellon on the same grounds. Harold Nicolson, Dwight Morrow (New York, 1935), 287.

representative to the Council.[3] Both McBride and Kublee would be invited later to join Morrow in Mexico and would influence his handling of Mexican-American relations.

In 1920 Morrow participated in the brief campaign to secure the Republican presidential nomination for Coolidge. He had mixed emotions when the latter was chosen Warren G. Harding's vice-presidential running mate. Morrow believed that Coolidge would make an excellent president but could find no serious fault with Harding.

The first few years of the new decade found Morrow involving himself in several vital international problems, such as European reconstruction, Allied war debts, and German reparations. The Morgan firm was involved in reconstruction loans to France, Italy, Great Britain, Belgium and Japan. Morrow familiarized himself with the problems faced by these nations and through his expertise contributed to their financial rehabilitation. Because of its position in the international financial community, Morgan & Company shunned the isolationism that seemed to permeate so many influential American circles in the postwar era. Morrow vehemently attacked the "holier than thou" attitude he felt many American politicians were taking toward Europe. He saw it as short-sighted and contrary to the best interest

---

[3] Ibid., 203-204; Mrs. Lewis B. McBride to author, August 17, 1974.

of the world community.[4]

In 1922 Morrow arranged two loans for the Cuban government. Cuba had sunk to new depths of fiscal irresponsibility as a result of a corrupt and inefficient administration and a sudden slump in 1921 in the sugar crop. Cuba had defaulted on debts owed the United States government and private American interests. There were many calls for an invocation of the Platt Amendment and intervention to bring order to Cuba's financial chaos. The loans ended the immediate crisis. Morrow also formulated a plan for the long-range rehabilitation of Cuban finances. From his involvement in Cuba's financial affairs, Morrow gained an appreciation of Latin Americans that was rare in American diplomatic circles and would serve him well in Mexico.[5]

In late 1925, Morrow again answered a call to public service, albeit a brief one, when he served as chairman of the Aircraft Board inquiry into Colonel William Mitchell's highly publicized charges that the national defense of the United States was compromised because of an inadequate and mismanaged Air Service. Morrow conducted the investigation and hearings in his typically efficient, no-nonsense manner. Expertly resolving differences among the members of the

---

[4] Nicolson, Dwight Morrow, 241-245.

[5] Ibid., 260-266. For full discussion of the Cuban loans see Dana G. Munro, The United States and the Caribbean Republics, 1921-1933 (Princeton, 1974), 16-43.

board, Morrow succeeded in drawing up a report which recognized the differences between the "old" and the "new" approaches to national defense. It suggested ways of alleviating the tensions between the proponents of the conflicting philosophies. Although Morrow believed that Mitchell had overstated his case, the report's recommendations reflected Morrow's opinion that airplanes were weapons to be reckoned with in all future conflicts. Upon the Board's recommendation the Air Service was renamed the Air Corps and new assistant secretaries were appointed to the War and Navy departments. Their primary activities were to center around aviation.[6]

The publicity given to Mitchell's allegations and the inquiry placed Morrow's name in the public spotlight and partially removed the limitations his association with J.P. Morgan & Company imposed upon his political and diplomatic aspirations. His friendship with McBride was renewed during the investigation when the latter served as his assistant.

Kellogg and Coolidge apparently approached Morrow in the spring of 1927 to learn whether he would be receptive to an offer of the Mexican ambassadorship. Morrow's response was affirmative.[7] He had been a great success with the Morgan firm making many friends and a great deal of money for

---

[6]Nicolson, Dwight Morrow, 280-287.

[7]Ellis, Frank B. Kellogg, 48.

himself and the firm. Yet a desire to try his hand at
politics or diplomacy made him increasingly dissatisfied
with his role as an investment banker.[8]

Coolidge evidently had overcome any hesitancy Morrow
might have expressed toward taking the post in Mexico City
by promising to give his former classmate considerable freedom of action. Reportedly the President told Morrow that
the only instruction he would give him would be to do "everything you honorably can to prevent war."[9] Coolidge expressed
his philosophy to Morrow, saying "it was not the business of
government to do good but to prevent harm." He felt that Morrow "probably could prevent a good deal of harm" if he went
to Mexico. The primary problem for the United States in its
relations with Mexico, Coolidge told Morrow, was "to find
some modus vivendi for getting along" with the Mexicans.
Probably with Sheffield in mind, Coolidge confided to Morrow that it was not "easy to get people with the equipment
and character" to get along with the Mexicans.[10]

Coolidge offered the post to Morrow formally on July
20, 1927, only six days after Sheffield tendered his resignation. Morrow accepted almost immediately, although he
would not be officially appointed until September 21. Shef-

---

[8] Nicolson, Dwight Morrow, 225, 247.

[9] Williams, "Reminiscences," II, 704.

[10] Morrow to J.P. Morgan, August 31, 1927, Morrow Papers.

field had 60 days leave left, and Morrow required time to conclude some of his own business matters. Morrow's partners attempted to dissuade him from taking the position. Lamont, Morrow's closest friend at Morgan & Company, urged him to decline because he saw "no liklihood[sic] of any definitive accomplishment in the next 18 months." He believed that the pending Mexican presidential campaign would precipitate turmoil, making his task impossible. He did not want his friend to become mired in such a futile endeavor.[11]

Lamont's pessimism undoubtedly had its genesis in the almost certain breakdown of the Lamont-Pani agreement. The trouble there stemmed from the declining revenues from oil production and oil export taxes. Calles' stubborn adherence to the provisions of the petroleum law reduced revenues from that source by about 16 percent in 1926.[12] The commitments under the Lamont-Pani accord for 1926 had been met only by borrowing from the Committee and the Bank of Mexico. Revenues for 1927 unquestionably would decline even more dramatically and were certain to kill the accord.[13]

Only an immediate resolution of the numerous outstanding conflicts between the two nations would allow for the

---

[11]Lamont to Morrow, August 5, 1927, ibid.

[12]Turlington, Mexico and Her Foreign Creditors, 312 fn.

[13]Lamont to Thomas Cochran, Arthur M. Anderson and Vernon Munroe, July 11, 1927, Morrow Papers. Revenues from oil production and export taxes declined from 35 million pesos in 1926 to 19 million in 1927. Turlington, Mexico and Her Foreign Creditors, 312 fn.

salvation of the 1925 agreement or the conclusion of a new accord acceptable to all. Lamont did not believe that such a resolution was on the horizon despite assurances from Pani that the outstanding questions would be settled after the anticipated election of Obregón as Calles' successor.[14]

Lamont responded to feelers put out by the Calles' government regarding the possibility of still another modification of the agreement between Mexico and the Committee by indicating that "an effective settlement of the outstanding and constantly irritating land and oil questions" was a prerequisite to discussion as to changes in the earlier accord. The importance of thse issues to Mexican-American relations made such discussions futile so long as the issues remained unresolved.[15]

Morrow's decision to accept the Mexican post was not altered by Lamont's fears or advice. Morrow was perfectly aware of the complexities of Mexican-American relations and of the numerous pitfalls that could be expected in the months ahead. Frequently Lamont, in his capacity as Chairman of the International Committee, had discussed with Morrow his difficulties in achieving some enduring agreement with Mexico. On several occasions Morrow conducted discussions with Mex-

---

[14] Lamont to Cochran, Anderson, Munroe, July 11, 1927, Morrow Papers.

[15] Lamont to Augustin Legorreta, July 15, 1927, ibid.

ican representatives in lieu of Lamont when the latter was abroad. Morrow obviously took the ambassadorship under no misapprehensions.

Within two days after he had accepted the post, Morrow began to receive briefings from the State Department. It was Undersecretary of State Olds (promoted to that position from Assistant Secretary on July 1, 1927) who first informed Morrow of current American policy toward Mexico. This policy had been formulated by Olds with Kellogg's approval.

Three months before Morrow left for Mexico City, Olds sent him a lengthy confidential memorandum in which he outlined the underlying philosophy behind American policy toward Mexico. He explained that despite continuous pressure on the part of "aggrieved parties" for the United States to "play the high hand," intervention was firmly rejected as a matter of policy. Whenever force had been used in the past, Olds pointed out, it made "the whole situation worse." Other drastic steps, such as lifting of the arms embargo or the severing of diplomatic relations, were also unacceptable since they could very well precipitate another revolution. The petroleum interests had inquired, Olds revealed, whether the lifting of the arms embargo could not be used to obtain concessions from the Mexican government. The Department informed them in no uncertain terms that national policy would not be "mortgaged" in that manner. "It would add little or nothing" to the American position "to threaten the use of force."[16]

Olds elaborated further on the new approach to Mexican-American relations that he had been instrumental in effecting and which he hoped that Morrow would implement. The policy would take into account "a shifting situation" and be "elastic enough to adapt itself to circumstances." For the first time in the unhappy history of relations between the two neighbors, "all points in the controversy" were being defined so that the Mexican government would know precisely where the American government stood on the issues, thus minimizing the chance for misunderstanding. The State Department was "patiently trying out" the theory that more could be achieved by telling the Mexicans what was expected of them and then giving them a chance to do it on their own than by insulting or forcing them. The United States was leaving the way open for the Mexican government "to find the way out of its difficulties by appropriate action of the legislative, executive, and judicial branches...acting on their own initiative."[17]

Olds boasted that this diplomatic approach had thus far been successful in that the "predictions of disaster have

---

[16] Olds to Morrow, Memorandum entitled "Mexico," July 22, 1927, ibid.

[17] Ibid.

not materialized." While it might be some time before Mexican-American relations took a turn for the better, the policy was justified by the fact that under it the situation had not appreciatively deteriorated. Despite heavy criticism from many quarters, this approach seemed to be "the only policy that fits the case." The alternatives, Olds maintained, were not "alluring."[18]

The policy outlined by Olds meshed well with Morrow's own inclinations. Morrow was a man of reason who preferred friendly, open discussions as a means of reconciling differences to coercion and threats. His experience with the Cubans and his respect for the personal dignity of all human beings rendered him ideally suited to implement the kind of policy Olds had described. Morrow was not handicapped by the feelings of superiority, racism, or the irrational fear of Mexican "bolshevism" that had so tragically limited Sheffield. At every juncture, Morrow would prove himself to be a realist. He found little difficulty in working harmoniously with Olds, who epitomized the same qualities in the State Department.

Just prior to Morrow's departure for Mexico City, Olds provided Morrow with another confidential memorandum dealing with the specific areas of friction between the two nations. Olds pointed out that the oil controversy was para-

---

[18]Ibid.

lyzing the industry and hurting Mexico. It was recommended that Morrow "work out a *modus vivendi*" which would enable oil production to go on and would provide the revenue that Mexico so desperately needed. Although this would be but a temporary solution, it would be helpful until a final settlement of the controversy could be reached, "either by a decision of the Mexican Supreme Court or otherwise."[19]

In regard to the land issue, Olds indicated that the Department had thus far found no satisfactory way of dealing with Mexico's agrarian policy, one which can "perhaps not be seriously controverted by us." Yet Olds wrote that the "real complaint" was not the policy itself but rather abuses that had crept in to the enforcement of the laws-- bonds were not being issued nor was cash being paid for the confiscated land as required by Mexican legislation. Olds suggested to Morrow that the situation could be "vastly improved" if he could prevail upon the Mexican government to make a "sincere attempt" to abide by its own laws.[20]

Olds also expressed hope that Morrow could persuade the Mexican government to cease from inhibiting the efforts of the two commissions that had been set up to consider the validity of claims against Mexico dating back to 1911. To date the Special Claims Commission and the General Claims

---

[19] Confidential Memorandum, Olds to Morrow, October 10, 1927, *ibid*.

[20] *Ibid*.

Commission had made little or no progress in the resolution of the numerous claims. Perhaps the two commissions could be merged, Olds suggested, and one presiding commissioner chosen to facilitate progress.[21]

In addition to these expressions of State Department policy and recommendations furnished by Olds, Morrow also received advice and intelligence from several other quarters prior to his departure for Mexico City. Lamont, in apparent anticipation that Morrow would be of assistance to the International Committee, brought his friend up to date as to the status of the Lamont-Pani agreement. He indicated that the policy of the Committee was "to hang on and press the [Mexican] Government to as complete a remittance as possible." Lamont expressed hope that the widespread publicity that had been given to the accord in 1925 would prevent the Mexicans from making a direct repudiation of it. If they did so, their hopes for future external credit would be fatally damaged.[22]

Additionally, Vernon Munroe, Secretary to the Committee, furnished Morrow with the latest figures regarding Mexico's 1928 obligations under the Lamont-Pani accord. This statement indicated that the total payments due from Mexico in 1928 amounted to $33.75 million. The anticipated revenues

---

[21] Ibid.

[22] Lamont to Morrow, September 23, 1927, ibid.

in 1927 from the oil taxes were expected to be approximately $12 million.[23] The 1928 revenues would undoubtedly be less.[24] How Mexico would make up the deficit was not clear, but it is likely that Lamont, like Olds, hoped that Morrow would achieve some understanding with Calles which would allow oil production to resume and improve revenues from that source significantly.

Morrow also received advice from former Ambassador Sheffield. Sheffield suggested to Morrow that he should pursue his policy of "firmness." The Mexicans, Sheffield confided, viewed any attempt at "modification or even conciliation where a principle of International Law is involved" as a sign of "weakness." He characterized his adversaries in Mexico as "extremely keen at reading your mind, clever in argument" and, he said, seldomly have they failed "to get the better of us in note writing." The "interminable note writing", Sheffield claimed, "led Mexico to feel that we were content with wordy protests and would not follow it [sic] up with any positive action."[25] Sheffield's advice, of course, was not only contrary to the State Department's "softer" policy, but it was also ill-suited to Mor-

---

[23] Munroe to Morrow, September 26, 1927, Box 19b, Lamont Papers.

[24] The actual revenues from oil production and export taxes in 1927 and 1928 were approximately $9.5 and $5.5 million, respectively. Turlington, Mexico and Her Foreign Creditors, 312 fn.

[25] Sheffield to Morrow, October 3, 1927, Morrow Papers.

row's personality.

Morrow departed for Mexico early in October 1927, after having severed his relationship with J.P. Morgan & Company, effective September 30. Controversy still raged in the United States and in Mexico concerning his appointment. Critics attacked the choice of a Morgan partner as a sign of a return to "dollar diplomacy." Many American newspapers editorially questioned the appropriateness of his appointment in view of the alleged Morgan interests in Mexico.[26] Morrow felt obliged in a letter to Kellogg to correct the inaccuracies of the critics' charges. He assured the Secretary that he had "no financial interest in the public debt of Mexico" and that while he had been a partner the Morgan firm had "issued no bonds of the Republic of Mexico, nor did they participate in any such issue of bonds." He contradicted contentions made in the press that J.P. Morgan & Company was a principal owner of the public debt of Mexico. He pointed out that in fact the firm owned but L15,900 in Mexican bonds.[27]

---

[26]The Lamont Papers contain a file of newspaper clippings from across the country in which Morrow's appointment was criticized editorially because of the allegedly heavy financial interest the Morgan firm had in Mexico. Lamont sent off long letters to the editors of each of the papers, whether large or small. Some of the papers he wrote to were: Kansas City Star, LaCrosse (Wisconsin) Tribune, and Emporia (Kansas) Gazette. He explained that J.P. Morgan & Company had no investment in Mexico and that Morrow no longer had any relationship with the firm. See Box 192, Lamont Papers.

[27]Morrow to Kellogg, October 18, 1927, Box 192, ibid.

While Morrow was journeying to Mexico City, Sheffield was predicting that no new policy could possibly occur under Morrow unless it was "towards...greater firmness and insistence on upholding American rights." While he claimed that, "There were many things we could and ought to do short of declaring war," Sheffield expressed concern that if the United States allowed things in Mexico to drift "into savagery, confiscation and chaos...then self-protection and self-respect" would require that that alternative be faced. It was clear that he both expected and looked forward to that kind of justification of his policies.[28]

Sheffield had praised Morrow's appointment as "wise." He believed that the Mexicans might temporarily succeed in deceiving Morrow but that eventually he would "see through the deceit and hypocrisy and understand the real hostility and Bolshevic tendencies that in reality control their national policies."[29] Sheffield had totally misjudged the character of his successor, although he claimed to know him well. He assumed that Morrow shared his feelings of superiority toward the Mexicans as well as his distrust of them.

Morrow presented his credentials to Calles' government on October 29, 1927. Calles used the occasion to tell Morrow privately that he felt many of the areas of conflict

---

[28] Sheffield to Julian S. Mason, October 21, 1927, Box 9, Sheffield Papers.

[29] Sheffield to Wadsworth, November 3, 1927, Box 9, ibid.

could be resolved through personal meetings. He expressed the opinion that diplomatic notes tended to drive governments further apart. He hoped that he and Morrow could settle amicably the differences between their governments. Morrow agreed to try personal discussions with the Mexican President as a means to bring about diplomatic agreement.[30]

On November 2, 1927, the ambassador breakfasted with Calles. Morrow quickly demonstrated himself to be sharply different from Sheffield. He demonstrated his trust in Calles by refusing to bring along his own interpreter, indicating that Calles' (who had been persona non grata at the American embassy under Sheffield) would do fine. Calles was impressed by this token gesture of goodwill. A basis for a new and happy relationship between the Ambassador and the Mexican president had its genesis in this subtle action. Discreetly Morrow avoided any discussion of controversial issues at this initial meeting.[31]

Calles was so impressed with Morrow that only a week later (November 8, 1927) he invited the ambassador for a second meeting. This occasion provided Morrow with the opportunity to study Calles and to learn his views on some of the important issues. Morrow liked the Mexicans. He reported to Kellogg that he was impressed by Calles'

---

[30] Morrow to Kellogg, November 8, 1927, Morrow Papers.
[31] Ibid.

"strength, his earnestness, and his apparent sincerity." Morrow felt that Calles was "capable of going a long way in either the right or wrong direction." He was optimistic that Calles would do the right thing. Morrow pointed out that most businessmen in Mexico felt that Calles was a better administrator than Obregón and was more faithful to his word than the former president.[32] Morrow's positive comments were in sharp contrast to the stream of negativism that emanated from the American embassy under Sheffield.

It was at this second meeting that Calles asked Morrow how he felt the oil controversy might be resolved. Morrow replied that he was a lawyer and viewed the problem in legal terms. Morrow suggested that if, in cases pending before it, the Mexican Supreme Court sustained its decision in the Texas Oil Company case of 1921, the "ground would be cleared for a satisfactory adjustment of the oil matter." The 1921 decision declared government attempts to establish control over subsoil petroleum rights retroactively to be unconstitutional.

Calles indicated that the petroleum law of 1925 was a political expediency intended to placate the "extreme radical wing" in Mexico at the time. There had never been any intention to confiscate the properties of the oil companies. The government needed the oil revenues. Confiscation would

---

[32] Ibid.

have been "suicide." The 50-year concessions, Calles felt, were the equivalents of perpetual rights. He was astounded that the oil companies had reacted so vehemently to this requirement. He implied that the blatant threat on the part of the oil interests to refuse to obey the Mexican law necessitated a firm stance on his part or he would lose face.

Anxious to settle the controversy, Calles asked if a Supreme Court decision in line with the Texas Oil case would settle the "main controversy" in the oil dispute. Morrow indicated that it would. Calles responded that such a decision would be forthcoming in two months.[33]

On November 17, 1927, the oil controversy was virtually resolved when the Mexican Supreme Court, as Calles had promised, issued a decision that drilling permits could not be cancelled for oil lands on which the owners had not performed "positive acts" merely because those owners had not applied for the 50-year concessions as required by Article 15 of the Petroleum Law of 1925. The rationale behind the decision was that the owners of these lands possessed oil "rights" not merely "expectancies" and that these rights could not be restricted. The "confirmation" of these rights "did not modify them, but...recognizes them."[34] Morrow believed that

---

[33] Ibid.

[34] See J. Reuben Clark, Jr., "The Oil Settlement with Mexico," Foreign Affairs, VI (July 1928), 609-610, for a fuller discussion of the decision.

this decision, while not resolving the whole oil question, dealt with "the most important question at issue."[35] On December 26, 1927, Calles recommended to the Mexican Congress that the petroleum law be amended to reflect the court's decision.

There were still difficult times ahead for the ambassador on this vital issue because of mutual suspicion between the oil companies and the Mexican government. Still, the quick progress Morrow had made towards resolution of the longstanding controversy was considered remarkable by the State Department, as was the overall improvement in relations between the embassy and the Calles government. From the Department the ambassador received nothing but praise and encouragement. Policymakers were undoubtedly pleased that at last there was a man in Mexico City who could be relied upon to implement the "softer" policy that had been decided upon. Olds wrote Morrow in response to his first report that, "you are on the right track and have already made real progress." In a slap at Sheffield, the Undersecretary bluntly stated that, "it delights us all to see the old method of long-armed dealing scrapped, and the contrary method of direct personal contact tried." He expressed confidence that "the lines along which you are working are absolutely sound."[36]

---

[35] Morrow to Lamont, January 3, 1928, Morrow Papers.
[36] Olds to Morrow, November 16, 1927, *ibid*.

Olds revealed the impact of Morrow's early successes on the Department. "The rapid swing in the right direction since your arrival," he confided soon after Calles promised a favorable Supreme Court decision, "has created an entirely new atmosphere in the Department and outside. We can not avoid a feeling of real optimism for the first time in years."[37]

Two weeks later Olds again felt compelled to congratulate Morrow. "Everybody feels that your methods and approaches are exactly right." Yet Olds was aware that the complex oil controversy could not be entirely resolved so quickly. He assured Morrow that there would be "no glib talk about sudden settlements from here. We realize that the problem in all its phases has to be worked out gradually and patiently." Olds then restated the Department's policy toward Mexico. "Somehow we are going to get along with Mexico, and everybody in Washington, from the President on down, has implicit confidence in your ability to secure the best results that the actual conditions from time to time permit."[38]

The Mexican congress moved rapidly and amended the petroleum law to reflect the Supreme Court's decision on December 29, 1927. Less than two weeks later, on January 9, 1928, Calles signed a bill amending the petroleum law by providing that the pre-constitutional vested rights to land

---

[37] Olds to Morrow, November 29, 1927, ibid.
[38] Olds to Morrow, December 9, 1927, ibid.

on which "positive acts" had been performed should be confirmed through the issuance of confirmatory concessions without time limitations.[39] Still, the oil companies were dissatisfied.

These companies feared that by applying for the confirmatory concessions they would be in danger of forfeiting their rights to land on which no "positive acts" had been performed. This was particularly true in cases where the properties lay within the zones prohibited by the law--the lands within 100 kilometers of Mexico's frontiers and 50 kilometers of its coast. They also feared that to submit to Mexican law would endanger their properties elsewhere in Latin America. The companies, therefore, continued to deny the right of the Mexican government to review the validity of their titles.[40]

Morrow was clearly annoyed by the rigid stance of the oil interests. He found the oil company representatives in Mexico City to be "most reasonable and helpful" but to have "little influence" on their employers in New York. The representatives appreciated the very real progress that had been made on the oil issues but company officials in the United States were dissatisfied. Morrow expressed surprise that they spent so much time complaining about what the oil

---

[39] Clark, "The Oil Settlement," 610-611. Application for the confirmatory concessions had to be made by January 11, 1929.

[40] W.L. Mellon to Morrow, April 11, 1928, Morrow Papers.

decision "did not do" instead of concentrating on "what the decision did do."[41] Morrow was indignant that they expected the State Department to uphold them in their insistence that no confirmation of their concessions was acceptable. He irreverently suggested that they should "go back into the oil business instead of trying to teach international law to all Latin America."[42] The ambassador firmly believed that Calles had yielded as much as he could on the issue and that it was dangerous for the oil companies to insist that he go still further.

An exchange of letters between Hilarion N. Branch, the representative of the Huasteca Petroleum Company, and Luis Morones, Secretary of Industry, Commerce and Labor, reaffirmed Mexico's good faith. Branch asked Morones, whose department was responsible for the administration of the petroleum law, whether a foreign oil company would surrender any of its rights held prior to May 1, 1917, when it applied for a confirmatory concession. Morones responded that a petition for confirmatory concessions did not imply the renunciation of those pre-constitutional rights.[43]

---

[41] Morrow to Lamont, January 3, 1928, ibid.

[42] Morrow to Olds, May 8, 1928; Morrow to Owen D. Young, April 6, 1928, both in ibid.

[43] Both letters quoted in Morrow to Kellogg, January 9, 1928, FRUS 1928, III, 294. For discussion of the significance of the Branch-Morones correspondence see Clark, "The Oil Settlement," 611.

It remained for the petroleum regulations to be modified to "harmonize" with the amendments to the petroleum law. The regulations, as originally written, defined "positive act" much more narrowly than did the Bucareli agreements. J. Reuben Clark Jr., Morrow's expert on the oil question, worked closely with representatives of Minister Morones to draft amendments to the regulations which would bring them into harmony with the amended petroleum law. This was accomplished by using the precise language employed by the Mexican commissioners at the Bucareli talks to define what constituted a "positive act," thus broadening the definition in the regulations.[44] On March 27, 1928, Calles signed the amended regulations.

The question of "untagged" lands (lands on which no "positive act" had been performed) remained unsettled since neither the amended law nor any other regulations made mention of this category of holdings. Morrow had concluded that if the oil companies had ever had a legal right to these subsoil deposits, then they probably continued to have that right. Yet he was skeptical of the legality of the companies' claims. Clark, who was assigned to study the entire oil ques-

---

[44]Morrow to Kellogg, March 6, 1928, FRUS 1928, III, 298-299 and Morrow to Kellogg, March 27, 1928, ibid., 300-301. Text of "Mexican Decree of March 27, 1928, containing amendments of the petroleum regulations promulgated April 8, 1928" is in ibid., 301-306.

tion, had come to believe that under Mexican law American companies could not successfully press their claims. Morrow was impressed by Clark's evidence.[45]

The State Department served notice to the oil companies in a press release issued on March 27, 1928, that they must not look to the Department for a resolution of this question. It stated that any additional questions that may arise should be settled through the "due operations of the Mexican administrative departments and the Mexican courts."[46]

Morrow's success in bringing about an apparent solution to the decade-old oil controversy without causing the Mexican government to lose face won him Calles' respect and trust. Morrow used the goodwill as a base from which to tackle the other areas of friction between the two nations. To assist him in the difficult months ahead and to bolster his staff, Morrow invited Lewis B. McBride (now a Captain in the Navy) and George Rublee to Mexico.

McBride was "loaned" to Morrow as a naval attache assigned to the embassy in Mexico.[47] In actuality, McBride devoted his attentions almost exclusively to financial matters including the public debt of Mexico, the agrarian debt and

---

[45] Morrow to Olds, April 3, 1928, Morrow Papers.

[46] Statement issued to the press by the Department of State, March 27, 1928, FRUS 1928, III, 307-308.

[47] Morrow to McBride, December 13, 1927, Morrow Papers; Mrs. McBride to author, August 17, 1974.

Mexican government budgets.[48] McBride quickly mastered Mexico's financial condition in all its complexity and Morrow soon came to rely heavily on him in this area.[49]

Rublee, a Washington attorney, had great admiration for Morrow, dating back to their World War I work, and he also had a fascination for diplomacy. Rublee had volunteered his services to the ambassador soon after Morrow was appointed. Only his precise role had to be worked out. By December 1927 Rublee was acting in an informal capacity as a liaison between the International Committee and Morrow.[50] In March 1928 he was formally added to the staff of the embassy as a legal adviser.[51] He too soon involved himself in untangling Mexico's financial affairs.

By his own admission Morrow devoted most of his attention in his first few months in Mexico to the oil question and "practically no time" to financial questions. He justified this to Lamont on the grounds that "So much of the revenue of the Government is dependent upon oil" that a resolution of the oil controversy might bring "some increase in revenue."[52] The validity of this contention is apparent when

---

[48] Stokely W. Morgan to Morrow, May 29, 1929, Morrow Papers.

[49] George Rublee, "The Reminiscences of George Rublee," (Oral History Research Office, Columbia University, New York, 1951), 216-217.

[50] Rublee to Morrow, December 31, 1927, Morrow Papers.

[51] Rublee, "Reminiscences," 211.

[52] Morrow to Lamont, January 3, 1928, Morrow Papers.

the percentage of government revenue derived from the oil production and export taxes is examined. In 1922, 30.16 percent of the government's revenues came from the oil taxes. By 1924 the figure had declined to 19.2 percent. In 1926, it was only 10.08 percent. For the first eight months of 1927 these taxes accounted for only 4.53 percent of government income.[53] Clearly the resolution of the oil question would significantly improve government income.

Prior to Morrow's coming to Mexico, Calles had discussed Mexico's finances candidly in a speech before the Mexican Congress. He had promised that his government intended to "cover scrupulously the public debt service," but he cautioned that this could be done only "so long as the economic capacity of the country does not necessitate that another road be taken." He revealed that although the Mexican treasury was in a "critical state" and a delay in the payments on the interior debt was necessary, the payments due under terms of the Lamont-Pani accord had been met through June 1927. He admitted that two loans from the International Committee totalling approximately $2.7 million were needed in January and July of 1927 to pay the interest on the National Railways debt for the last half of 1926 and the charges on the foreign debt for the first half of 1927. This

---

[53] Report of the Naval Attaché, December 6, 1927, Records of the Office of the Chief of Naval Operations, Office of Naval Intelligence. National Archives, Record Group 38.

state of affairs Calles blamed on the dramatic decline in revenues from the petroleum taxes.[54]

Lamont had kept Morrow informed through the last months of 1927 on the steady deterioration in Mexico's financial outlook. The picture certainly was bleak. Oil production for the first nine months of 1927 declined by 31 percent from a comparable period in 1926. The combined revenues from the oil production and export taxes declined by 45 percent in the same period.[55] Estimates of anticipated revenues from the petroleum taxes for 1928 were considered so unreliable that the proposed budget for 1928 did not include this source of income. One government estimate was that the oil taxes would bring in approximately 20 million pesos. The oil men calculated revenues of about 16 million pesos. Whatever the amount, it would be applied toward the public debt.[56] There was no hope that Mexico would be able to honor in full its debt liabilities for 1928, which amounted to approximately $26.5 million.

In view of these facts, Calles sent representatives to New York in late 1927 to discuss with the International Committee the possibility of a new agreement which would re-

---

[54] Calles' Message to the Mexican Congress, September 1, 1927, in Murray, Mexico Before the World, 177-178.

[55] Munroe to Morrow, November 22, 1927, Box 196, Lamont Papers.

[56] Report of the Naval Attaché, February 14, 1928.

flect more realistically Mexico's current income. The Committee, upon Morrow's recommendation, concluded that a new agreement would be doomed to failure unless a careful study of Mexico's financial condition was made. It was agreed that Mexico would pay in the first six months of 1928 the arrears for 1927 but would suspend payments for 1928 until the study was completed.[57] It was decided that Joseph E. Sterrett of Price, Waterhouse & Company, and Professor Joseph S. Davis of Stanford University, would journey to Mexico and, with the assistance of the Mexican officials, make a thorough study of Mexico's current financial circumstances, as well as a realistic estimate of the country's future capacity to pay.

Morrow had been suddenly cast into the unusual role of adviser to both the Calles government and the International Committee. Late in 1927, the Mexican president candidly had revealed to him the nation's fiscal plight and had asked for his assistance. The curious result was that Calles sent Minister of Finance Luis Montes de Oca, who had succeeded Pani in February 1927, to Morrow for advice in framing his replies to correspondence from the Committee.[58]

Morrow handled this potentially dangerous situation in a manner that proved advantageous to both sides. He was con-

---

[57] Morrow to Kublee, February 2, 1928, Morrow Papers.
[58] Ibid.

vinced that the obligations under the Lamont-Pani agreements for 1928 could not be met. He informed Lamont that he could not rely on any promises that the Mexican government might make regarding partial payment.[59] To Arthur Anderson, a Morgan partner, Morrow confided that "The real difficulty down here is that the Government is insolvent and doesn't know it yet."[60] He cautioned the Committee that "any new agreement at this time" would be "impracticable" since estimates of Mexico's capacity to pay even for the latter half of 1928 would be only "opinion." Morrow recommended that a thorough study of Mexico's finances be undertaken before any new agreement was made.[61] The Sterrett-Davis study was initiated as a result of this suggestion.

Lamont was pleased that Morrow was involving himself in the resolution of Mexican financial problems. He expressed optimism to J.P. Morgan that Morrow would be of "immeasurable value" and that finally there was "something more permanent to look forward to for the bondholders" than the earlier, "temporary" agreements that had been "designed to get

---

[59] Morrow to Lamont, January 3, 1928, ibid.

[60] Morrow to Anderson, January 8, 1928, ibid. The belief that Mexico was in fact "insolvent" was in the months ahead to become a major factor in Morrow's approach to Mexico's financial problems. In January 1928 Morrow probably had not yet developed fully his concept of "national insolvency," which would bring him into conflict with Lamont. There is no evidence that in early 1928 Lamont viewed Morrow's reference to Mexican "insolvency" as more than mere rhetoric.

[61] Morrow to Munroe, January 10, 1928, ibid.

as much money for the bondholders as could be legitimately secured."[62] Lamont's enthusiasm led him to write Morrow in Mexico that he was "in a fair way to do more than anyone has ever done there in the memory of man."[63]

Sterrett and Davis spent approximately three months (January through April 1928) in Mexico gathering first-hand information. They enjoyed the full assistance of the Mexican government and of Morrow and his staff. The Calles administration demonstrated its good faith by making available to the investigators all the data pertinent to their study.

The Sterrett-Davis report, submitted to the International Committee on May 25, 1928, has been praised by most authorities as a model of completeness and objectivity.[64] The report credited Mexico with having made "important strides economically and politically toward recovery from the devastation and disorganization of the revolutionary period." Yet Mexico had not yet achieved a level at which it could meet promptly its current expenses or honor fully the service on its debt. Mexico's financial debility had its genesis in a myriad of crises. Some of the events had long passed but had left behind them a legacy of financial instability.

---

[62]Lamont to Morgan, January 16, 1928, Box 192, Lamont Papers.

[63]Lamont to Morrow, February 10, 1928, Box 196, ibid.

[64]See for example, Wynne, State Insolvency, 77; Turlington, Mexico and Her Foreign Creditors, 314.

Others, whether old or recent in origin, continued to plague the national treasury. The political chaos that began in 1911 and, to a degree, still endured with periodic flare-ups occurring as recently as 1923, 1924 and 1927, was a constant drain on the nation's resources. The dramatic decline in receipts from oil taxes reduced the nation's income severely. The implementation of agrarian land reform measures required that new liabilities be assumed at a time when they could be ill-afforded. The long-standing friction between church and state tended to "unsettle confidence, reduce productivity, and make for unrest," all of which resulted in decreased revenues. Additionally, such well-intentioned social projects and services for Mexico's citizens as expanded educational opportunity and public works projects, combined to increase government expenditures at a time when income was on a decline.[65]

The report suggested that in view of Mexico's current financial condition it could only apply approximately 30 million pesos annually from its income to meet its debt service obligations. But prospects for increased income in the near future were good (particularly in view of recent understandings regarding the petroleum laws). As Mexico's income increased, the amount available to be applied to its debts

---

[65] Wynne, State Insolvency, 77-78; Morrow to Kellogg, August 3, 1928, Morrow Papers.

would also rise. Within three years at least 70 million pesos should be available for this purpose and in five years at least 90 million pesos would be available, barring some unexpected turn of events.[66]

The report pointed out, however, that the commitments made to the International Committee were not Mexico's only obligations. It also had liabilities in the form of a floating debt, bonds issued in pursuit of land reform measures, claims against it by foreigners for damages incurred during the numerous periods of domestic turmoil, as well as miscellaneous other internal obligations. To deal satisfactorily with these liabilities, it was recommended that a comprehensive plan be drawn up which would take into consideration all classes of obligations held by both Mexicans and foreigners--bonds, claims, floating debt, etc.--and that "suitable provision" be made for all interest arrears.[67]

Before the Calles government and the International Committee could digest the recommendations of the Sterrett-Davis report, events in Mexico took still another unexpected turn. On July 17, 1928 president-elect Alvaro Obregón was assassinated. Obregon was to have taken office on December 1, 1928. His murder, by a Catholic fanatic, was the climax of a long and bitter struggle between revolutionary leaders

---

[66]Wynne, State Insolvency, 78.

[67]Ibid.; Morrow to Kellogg, August 3, 1928, Morrow Papers.

and the Catholic Church in Mexico. The enactment of legislation in 1926 which implemented the anti-clerical provisions of the 1917 Constitution had brought swift reaction from the hierarchy of the Church. All church services were suspended. An economic boycott was imposed. Catholics were asked not to support the Calles government. The inevitable result was a still more volatile situation. In some Mexican states fanatics took up arms under the slogan "<u>Viva Cristo Rey</u>." Clashes with the Mexican military increased in frequency and spilled blood over the countryside. It was one of these "Cristeros" who had assassinated Obregon.

The murder of Obregon was a severe setback to the efforts of Morrow to effect a settlement of the church-state dispute. Even before he had come to Mexico, Morrow had talked with Father John J. Burke, the General Secretary of the National Catholic Welfare Conference, who requested that the ambassador ascertain whether Calles would meet with him to discuss a settlement of the controversy. Calles readily agreed and, after one postponement due to premature publicity, the two met and discussed the religious issues "in a broad and liberal way and without rancor." This was quite a departure from the excessive rhetoric of the past.[68]

Morrow had been optimistic that an understanding could

---

[68]Morrow to Kellogg, July 23, 1928, <u>FRUS 1928</u>, III, 326-328.

be reached between the two men which would enable a normalization of relations between church and state and provide a boost to Mexico's sagging economy. Calles had made it clear to Morrow soon after the latter's arrival in Mexico that he had no desire to interfere in the spiritual affairs of the church, but that he could not tolerate counter-revolutionary activity on the part of the clergy. He must and would enforce the laws prohibiting those activities.[69]

Burke and Calles exchanged letters in which a practical modus vivendi was spelled out for consideration by Burke's superiors. Unfortunately, the more intransigent prelates of Mexico applied pressure to the Vatican to refuse any understanding with Calles short of an amendment to the Constitution negating the offensive provisions and repeal of the legislation enforcing those conditions. Thus, the Vatican took a short-sighted and rigid position against the accommodation which Morrow was attempting to achieve. The Obregón assassination rendered his task hopeless for the time being.[70]

Also sidetracked by the assassination was Morrow's plan for checking the runaway land reform measures that had made

---

[69] Morrow to Olds, December 9, 1927, Morrow Papers.

[70] Morrow to Kellogg, July 23, 1928, FRUS 1928, III, 353-354. For a thorough discussion of Morrow's efforts see, L. Ethan Ellis, "Dwight Morrow and the Church-State Controversy in Mexico," Hispanic American Historical Review, XXXVIII, (November 1958), 482-505.

budget projections mere guess work and economic stability impossible. The constitution had called for the expropriation of private holdings (largely from foreigners) which were to be redistributed to the peons. Compensation at the rate of 110 percent of the assessed value of the land expropriated was to be paid the owners in the form of five percent bonds maturing in 20 years. Landowners claimed that their land was assessed far below its true value and that it was in effect being confiscated. Issuance of bonds was very slow, and this too further aggravated the hard feelings between the owners and the government.

Since expropriation followed no systematic, controlled procedure but was swept along by a revolutionary fervor that varied in intensity from year to year and even from month to month, the Mexican Minister of Finance could not know what obligations the nation would be assuming in the upcoming months from the issuance of still more agrarian bonds. Thus each Mexican budget was, of necessity, highly imprecise. By 1930, when the issuance of these agrarian bonds was halted, approximately 24.5 million pesos in principal amount had been issued. This figure represented compensation for only about four percent of the land expropriated.[71] About 12.5 percent of all the land expropriated was taken from

---

[71] Eyler N. Simpson, The Ejido: Mexico's Way Out (Chapel Hill, N.C., 1937), 221.

foreigners, of which approximately 37.5 percent came from Americans.[72]

Morrow's background and training made him skeptical of the wisdom of any government interference in the private sector. On the other hand, Morrow was sympathetic to the plight of the peon and recognized that the tide of agrarian reform could not be reversed.[73] He therefore attempted a pragmatic approach to the question. His friendship with Calles gave him reason to believe that the Mexicans would see that justice ruled in specific cases of discrimination or confiscation. Thus he handled each claim by an American citizen individually and refused to pursue claims he deemed improper. Legitimate instances of injustice were resolved informally with Mexican authorities. Sometimes it was recommended that claims be pursued in the Mexican courts and on other occasions that they be submitted to a claims commission.[74] In this manner Morrow protected the property rights of Americans without offending revolutionary sensibilities. The ambassador's long-range goal was to find some practical solution to the problem of agrarian reform so that it could proceed in some kind of controlled manner. Expropriations then would not exceed Mexico's capacity to pay. Discriminatory and confiscatory practices would end. Land could be more

---

[72] Turlington, Mexico and Her Foreign Creditors, 310 fn, 311.

[73] Morrow to Olds, December 9, 1927, Morrow Papers.

[74] "Memorandum Relating to the Agrarian Situation in Mexico," no date, ibid.

quickly restored to cultivation of the crops Mexico so desperately needed. Obregón's untimely death postponed any hope for such a plan.

The assassination threw Mexico in a turmoil and placed all Morrow's plans in abeyance. The ambassador could not even speculate as to what the situation would be on any of the issues. He wrote Kellogg that the assassination placed a "very heavy burden" upon Calles. Although Morrow felt certain that Calles no longer wanted the presidency, he asked rhetorically, "who is to take his place?" Morrow was a keen observer of Mexican affairs, with a remarkable insight into the personalities of its leaders, but he also acknowledged that it was "too early to say what the outcome [of the domestic turmoil] will be."[75]

---

[75] Morrow to Kellogg, July 23, 1928, FRUS 1928, III, 334.

CHAPTER V

DISAGREEMENT BETWEEN MORROW AND LAMONT

The assassination of president-elect Obregón in July 1928 threw Mexico into a turmoil. Not only did the anti-Catholic reaction which followed the murder negate the détente towards which Morrow had been so carefully working, but the political and economic future of Mexico was clouded by still greater uncertainty. Obregón had been selected to succeed Calles when his term expired on November 30, 1928, as part of a political deal intended to safeguard the status quo. Obregón's death presented a dilemma for Calles. The constitution forbade a president from succeeding himself. Therefore, Calles must either step aside by December 1, or ignore the constitutional provision.

In the uncertainty that followed the assassination, Morrow suggested to Calles that perhaps the well-being of the nation demanded that he remain on as interim president until order could be restored and a satisfactory replacement found.[1] Calles indicated that he would abide by his pledge to step down. He had no wish to become a dictator.[2] Morrow was forced to agree that such an example would have many advantages for the nation. He refused to offer suggestions as to whom should succeed Calles. Morrow claimed that it would

---

[1] Morrow to Kellogg, August 14, 1928, Morrow Papers.
[2] Nicolson, *Dwight Morrow*, 344.

(143)

be "improper for an official of our Government to express a choice." He maintained that all the United States desired was that there be a "peaceful transfer of the government to anyone satisfactory to the Mexican people who was competent to carry on."[3]

The Obregón assassination cast another shadow over Mexico's tottering economy. It aroused further the anxieties of the International Committee. Although the Sterrett-Davis report was distinguished by its detail and precision, its data and projections were rendered questionable by the unexpected turn of events. Conditions had been altered substantively and a supplementary investigation was imperative.

Ironically, the report had had a far greater influence on Morrow and the Mexicans than it had on the Committee that had authorized it. The report's primary recommendation--that a comprehensive plan dealing with all of Mexico's outstanding debts be drawn up--fell on deaf ears in New York. The Committee's approach long had been "to get as much money for the bondholders as could be legitimately secured."[4] Like Mexico's other creditors, the Committee had negotiated agreements without regard to the other classes of debts owed. It operated on the premise that each group of creditors should and would look after its own interests. It was assumed

---

[3] Morrow to Kellogg, August 14, 1928, Morrow Papers.

[4] Lamont to Morgan, January 16, 1928, Box 192, Lamont Papers; Rublee, "Reminiscences," 215.

that the Committee owed it to those it represented to get all it could from Mexico before others beat them to it. To collect something now was better than vague promises of getting the entire amount at some future date.[5]

Morrow, on the other hand, was impressed greatly by the Sterrett-Davis report's recommendations. To a remarkable degree they coincided with the conclusions reached earlier by his own adviser on financial matters, Captain Lewis B. McBride. McBride had joined the embassy staff as a naval attache in early 1928. He was assigned to study the question of Mexican finances. Because of their eleven-year friendship, Morrow had complete faith in McBride's abilities. He relied heavily on him on questions concerning Mexico's debts and budgets.[6] The rigid stance Morrow would take for the remainder of his tenure in Mexico City regarding the Mexican debt was a direct result of McBride's influence.

In May 1928 McBride had outlined in a memorandum for Morrow an approach to the debt question that the ambassador quickly embraced in its entirety. Fundamentally, the philosophy and recommendations of the memorandum were identical to those offered by the Sterrett-Davis report a short

---

[5] Rublee to Morrow, December 31, 1927, Morrow Papers.

[6] Rublee, "Reminiscences," 216-217; Stokely W. Morgan to Morrow, May 29, 1929, Morrow Papers.

time later. The memorandum contended that a government which in peace time could not meet its obligations in full was analagous to a "commercial undertaking in temporary and voluntary receivership." Forced liquidation was, of course, out of the question since the nation would continue to exist as a political entity. Yet the condition of insolvency would seem to require taking extraordinary measures in the "interest of both debtor and creditor." Among these unusual steps the memorandum suggested that current creditors be paid in cash since the creation of new debt was inconsistent with successful financial rehabilitation. Small claims against the government should also be settled for cash in the interest of "administrative simplification." Similarly, holders of larger claims who were willing to liquidate their credits at "substantial" discounts should also be paid in cash.[7]

In regard to the Mexican debt as a whole, the memorandum suggested that when a nation could not meet the full service on its debt it was "very dangerous, and in most cases improper" for it to conclude separate settlements with "any particular class of creditors without taking into consideration the rights of other classes of creditors." This pell-mell approach is "nearly always justly open to

---

[7] "Memorandum on the Public Debt of Mexico," May 20, 1928, ibid.

suspicion and criticism on the grounds of favoritism, or worse." Only a comprehensive plan, taking into account all the various classes of creditors to which Mexico was obligated and granting each a fair share of the resources available for the debt service, could be of permanent value.[8]

The memorandum concluded on an optimistic note. It recognized that Mexico's present situation was "serious and could easily become unmanageable," but was hopeful that "sound and prompt steps" like those recommended could do "full justice" to all creditors without "imposing an undue strain on the country's resources and without too great sacrifices on the part of its citizens." As a happy by-product to such a scheme, Mexico's credit on the world's money markets would be reestablished.[9]

Morrow was convinced by the McBride memorandum and the Sterrett-Davis report that the methods used in the past by creditors were ill-suited to the realities of Mexico's financial condition.[10] Morrow could no longer support a separate agreement between Mexico and the International Committee, despite his long relationship with Lamont and the Morgan firm and his awareness of the difficulties encountered over the years by the Committee in protecting the bondhold-

---

[8]Ibid.

[9]Ibid.

[10]Rublee, "Reminiscences," 214-215.

ers it represented.

Once convinced of the correctness of his position, Morrow moved decisively. In discussions with President Calles and Minister of Finance Montes de Oca, Morrow stressed the futility of numerous separate agreements with creditors and the importance for Mexico of one comprehensive plan. The revelation to him by Montes de Oca that it was unlikely that Mexico would be able to pay any more in 1928 than the amounts owed to the Committee from 1926 and 1927, reaffirmed Morrow's belief that the stopgap approach was unworkable.[11]

On June 12, 1928, the Minister of Finance informed Lamont that Mexico could not meet the obligations due in 1928 under the Lamont-Pani agreement, although it would continue to make payments on the deficit for 1926 and 1927. Mexico would therefore be compelled to issue a decree suspending interest payments on the outstanding bonds.[12]

The Committee was disturbed greatly by the proposed decree. In Lamont's absence, Arthur Anderson warned that such a decree, "if unaccompanied by some constructive and definitive announcement," would have a "serious and disturbing effect" on the bondholders. It would negate what he claimed was the "generally held" impression that Mexico's

---

[11] "Memorandum of Conference with Montes de Oca on May 21, 1928," dated May 26, 1928, Morrow Papers; Morrow to Anderson, April 5, 1928, ibid.

[12] Montes de Oca to Lamont, June 12, 1928, ibid.

"political, commercial and financial affairs" were "tending toward a more normal position."[13]

Lamont objected even more strongly. He was "greatly distressed" by the proposed decree. He told Montes de Oca that the issuance of the decree would result in "serious injury to the credit of the Mexican Government" that neither he nor the Committee could prevent. He warned that the bondholders would "undoubtedly" take the declaration to be "tantamount to permanent repudiation" of the debt.[14] These statements were gross hyperbole since the bondholders and the investment community had experienced far too many disappointments in Mexico to be so disturbed by one more setback. Still the Mexican government was sufficiently intimidated by Lamont's remarks to abandon the proposed decree.[15]

Meanwhile, Morrow informed Kellogg that he was essentially in agreement with the recommendations of the Sterrett-Davis report and that he had been urging Calles and Montes de Oca to follow the report's recommendations as a path to financial stability. Morrow reported that since November 1927 he had been urging the Mexicans to pay all their current bills promptly. Since January 1, 1928, they had been following that policy. Morrow revealed that despite heavy

---

[13] Anderson to Montes de Oca, June 26, 1928, ibid.
[14] Lamont to Montes de Oca, July 10, 1928, ibid.
[15] Montes de Oca to Lamont, August 4, 1928, ibid.

pressure from some departments, Montes de Oca steadfastly had opposed expenditures in excess of budgeted limitations. This was done with the support of Calles. He intended to use any treasury surplus to pay salaries and overdue supply bills from past years.[16]

Morrow told Kellogg that a comprehensive plan was essential for Mexico's financial reconstruction. He argued that any revised or new accord concluded between Mexico and the International Committee should be part of such an *en bloc* agreement. This did not mean that priorities could be ignored but rather that "to a certain extent *all* creditors have an interest in any agreement with *any* creditors."[17] He had avoided broaching the subject of priorities with Mexican officials. These "difficult questions" could be decided at a later date.[18]

Morrow indicated to Kellogg that a successful comprehensive financial plan would have to be preceded by the adoption of a cash basis policy for any additional land taken in pursuit of the agrarian land reform program. He acknowledged that it would be politically very difficult for Mexico to change its agrarian policy but maintained that some modification in the mode of payment could be effected.[19]

---

[16] Morrow to Kellogg, August 3, 1928, *ibid*.

[17] *Ibid*.

[18] Morrow to Kellogg, July 31, 1928, *ibid*.

[19] Morrow to Kellogg, August 3, 1928, *ibid*.

Morrow had become increasingly convinced that Mexico was insolvent and that it was imperative that it and its creditors recognize that fact and act accordingly. McBride had sought historical precedent for the concept of "national insolvency." He had determined that the Egyptian bankruptcy of the late nineteenth century provided a precedent that could be followed in Mexico. Both McBride and Morrow studied the definitive work on the Egyptian financial problem and the solution found for it written by Evelyn Baring (Lord Cromer). Baring was the British representative to the Commission of Liquidation for the last quarter of the nineteenth century. Morrow and McBride were convinced that the same procedure could and should be applied to Mexico.[20] In Egypt, after twenty years' effort, a comprehensive agreement was concluded under a bankruptcy-like scheme. Egypt's creditors were grouped into classes based on the nature of the obligations held--secured, unsecured, long-term, short-term, other claims, floating debt, etc. All legitimate creditors shared in the available Egyptian resources on a class basis.[21]

The actual income for the first six months of 1928 exceeded the conservative estimates of Montes de Oca by 10.3

---

[20] Nicolson, Dwight Morrow, 386.

[21] See Evelyn Baring, Modern Egypt (2 vols., New York, 1908-1909) and Wynne, State Insolvency, 577-632. The Morrow Papers contain a copy of the final plan of liquidation for Egypt.

million pesos due to unexpected increased revenues from import and general stamp taxes. These funds were not applied to the foreign debt but were used to cover salary arrears and current supply bills as Morrow had suggested.[22] At the current rate Morrow estimated that another five years would be required before the floating debt was discharged. Morrow was certain that Mexico's other creditors would not tolerate long the application of excess funds to the floating debt. Soon they would be pressing Mexico to conclude new agreements by which they too would share in the higher revenues. Morrow intended that these new agreements be part of an *en bloc* settlement.[23]

The fluid state of the Mexican economy in mid-1928 was rendered more volatile by the Obregón assassination. This necessitated that the International Committee receive supplementary data to that included in the Sterrett-Davis report. Therefore, in the summer of 1928, Sterrett made two additional trips to Mexico to "ascertain the developments of the year 1928 in their relation to the finances of the Government of Mexico."[24]

---

[22] Unsigned memorandum (from internal evidence probably written by McBride), dated August 4, 1928, Morrow Papers; Morrow to Kellogg, August 5, 1928, ibid.

[23] Morrow to Kellogg, August 6, 1928, ibid.

[24] Joseph E. Sterrett, The Fiscal and Economic Condition of Mexico: Supplemental Report Dated November 15, 1928 (New York, 1928), 1. Copy in the Office of the Chief of Naval Operations, Office of Naval Intelligence, National Archives, Record Group 38.

153

Sterrett concluded that there was "not much chance of further payments to the Committee this year." Obregón's death had "checked the flow of business and the resulting uncertainty" would continue to reduce national income at least until the provisional president took office. Additionally, the internal turmoil which resulted from the assassination would "almost certainly" require new expenditures.[25]

Sterrett, like Morrow, emphasized once again the need for "a comprehensive plan under which both the Government and the Railways can have their debts organized so as to make the best use of their present limited funds and have a fair opportunity to develop their economic resources." He stressed the danger of making debt payments "here and there wherever the pressure gets to be the most severe and with little regard to the priority of the particular debt." Such an approach was short-sighted since "relief at one point brings pressure somewhere else" with little improvement in the debt situation.[26]

Sterrett was convinced that Mexico's financial condition was by "no means hopeless." But the "friendly assistance" of the International Committee would be needed for Mexico's rehabilitation since the Mexicans had limited experience in such tasks. He believed that administration of-

---

[25] Sterrett to Anderson, September 6, 1928, Morrow Papers.

[26] Ibid.

ficials were willing to learn and would welcome such assistance from those they recognized to be of "wider experience than their own."[27]

Revenues for 1928, Sterrett determined, probably would be at least as high as the revised estimate of 296.5 million pesos. Only about 24 million pesos would be available for application to the public debt. None would be available for payments due the Committee under the 1925 agreement.[28]

Sterrett judged the budget estimates for 1929 of slightly over 289 million pesos probably to be conservative in view of the under-estimates of 1927 and 1928. Similarly, the projected 29.9 million pesos earmarked for the public debt in 1929 was probably an underestimate.[29]

On September 10, 1928, the Mexican Finance Minister informed the International Committee that his government was "ready to confer with its creditors" in regard to the external public debt. He expressed hope that either a new agreement could be consummated or that a basis for a future agreement could be reached. Montes de Oca desired that it be understood prior to the negotiations that Mexico's current ability to pay must be taken into account. He expected that the agreement would cover both the principal and interest due on the outstanding bonds. The Minister insisted

---

[27] Ibid.
[28] Sterrett, Supplemental Report, 2.
[29] Ibid., 3.

that the administrative and financial rehabilitation of the Mexican National Railways be considered at the meetings together with the external debt questions since they constituted a joint problem for Mexico. He argued that the solution of these two problems would be "of the greatest advantage to Mexico and its creditors."[30]

Lamont responded affirmatively to Montes de Oca's overture. He agreed that any new agreement must reflect Mexico's capacity to pay. But he felt that Mexico's future capacity should also be taken into consideration. Lamont diplomatically expressed the opinion that conditions would "continue to improve under the wise hands of those now ruling your country's destinies."[31] It was agreed that representatives of the Committee would go to Mexico to discuss terms of a new agreement with Mexican officials.

In October 1928, Arthur Anderson and Sterrett went to Mexico on behalf of the International Committee. Under Morrow's influence, Montes de Oca insisted during the preliminary discussions that any new agreement be part of "a comprehensive plan that would include not only the settlement of the Direct External Debt, but likewise the organization and arrangement of the Internal Debt, the settlement and payment of claims of foreigners and the firm and definitive

---

[30] Montes de Oca to Lamont, September 10, 1928, Morrow Papers.

[31] Lamont to Montes de Oca, September 28, 1928, ibid.

balancing of the Budget." He was willing to accept "separate, but...integral" solutions for the various aspects of Mexico's financial problems as long as none of the partial solutions jeopardized the final settlement of the other facets.[32] The Committee indicated a willingness to accept these stipulations as a basis for a future agreement.

Morrow believed it would be difficult or impossible for a series of separate agreements to be in harmony with one another. He continued to campaign for one comprehensive plan. Candidly he told Lamont that he did not think that any partial settlement should be made with the Committee or any other group of creditors. Such partial settlements would "most inevitably break down and delay the real financial reorganization of the country." This was the reason he had refused to conclude an agreement with Mexico regarding claims of the United States government against it, despite suggestions from the Mexicans that such an agreement be made. This kind of "isolated transaction" would be of no value to the United States since it would be an agreement with an insolvent government and, more importantly, with a government "that was not made solvent" by the agreement.[33]

In late December 1928 Montes de Oca submitted to the Mexican Congress the draft of a law intended to be the initial step towards the formulation of a plan like the one

---

[32] Montes de Oca to Lamont, November 20, 1928, ibid.

[33] Morrow to Lamont, November 29, 1928, ibid.

discussed with the International Committee. It was ratified quickly and signed by the president on January 25, 1929. The law called for the suspension of payments of principal and interest on all internal obligations (with the exceptions of the agrarian and Carranza banking debts). A special <u>Comisión Adjustadora</u> was to be created to receive and pass judgment on internal claims against the government. Obligations under the Lamont-de la Huerta and Lamont-Pani agreements of 1922 and 1925, respectively, were to be subject to a new agreement. This new accord would consolidate these debts in exchange for new bonds redeemable in not less than 45 years and bearing an annual interest rate of not more than five percent. National Railway obligations would be negotiated separately. Claims by foreign governments could be settled, at the discretion of the president, by lump-sum payments.[34]

Morrow steadfastly opposed the understanding arrived at between Montes de Oca and the Committee and the definitive agreement towards which they were working. In this opposition he had the unwavering support of the State Department. Kellogg told Morrow that the Department had not been consulted regarding the negotiations nor advised of their nature.[35] Lamont was aware of Morrow's opposition to the plan and therefore for the first time since the Committee's

---

[34] Wynne, <u>State Insolvency</u>, 78-80; Turlington, <u>Mexico and Her Foreign Creditors</u>, 316.

[35] Kellogg to Morrow, November 2, 1928, <u>FRUS 1928</u>, III, 321.

foundation ceased to consult with the State Department before entering into negotiations, possibly because of the high regard within the Department for Morrow's opinion.

Kellogg informed Morrow that the Department did not desire at that time to take any formal position on the negotiations. However, Morrow was asked to remind the Mexican government that there were other American creditors besides those represented by the International Committee and that they should not be overlooked when "financial adjustments" were made. The State Department was not prepared yet to discuss the "relative priorities" of various Mexican obligations held by American citizens or others. The Department believed that Mexico's obligation to compensate American citizens for "property appropriated or destroyed, or for life lost, or for arrest and imprisonment, or for a personal assault in Mexico" was not "inferior" to obligations owed to those who had "voluntarily lent money to Mexico upon the faith of a bond."[36]

Kellogg advised Morrow that the Department would "carefully consider" whether under Mexico's existing financial condition, it should not "earnestly protest" any new arrangement with a particular group of creditors which appears to constitute "an undue or unfair preference in favor of such creditors to the detriment of other American creditors of

---

[36]Ibid., 321-322.

equal rank."[37]

With this firm support from the Department, Morrow frequently and frankly expressed his distaste for the proposed agreement to both Montes de Oca and the International Committee. He informed the Mexicans that an "unfortunate situation would arise" if a new agreement was concluded regarding the external bonded debt which by its very nature might break down if Mexico was faced with the need to meet its other obligations, including claims by foreign governments.[38] Morrow reportedly suggested that Mexico wait one year before signing the accord.[39]

To Vernon Munroe, Secretary of the Committee, Morrow bluntly stated his concern. "I regret that the International Committee still feels it desirable to have a contract rather than to use its great influence in assisting the Mexican Government in the formation of a program." Morrow acknowledged that in following this course, the Committee was merely doing what had been done by others. But, he pointed out, the result would be that none of the agreements could be relied upon. The only way that Mexico could honor the type of agreement that was being discussed would be to break agreements it had with other creditors.[40]

───────────

[37] Ibid., 323.

[38] Morrow to Kellogg, November 9, 1928, ibid., 322-323.

[39] Anderson to Lamont, January 2, 1929, Box 192, Lamont Papers.

[40] Morrow to Munroe, February 26, 1929, Morrow Papers.

The International Committee attempted to negate the impact of Morrow's warnings to the Mexicans. In early January 1929 Augustin Legorreta, who was functioning as a liaison between the Committee and the Mexican government, agreed to try to "induce" Morrow not to "press [his] views on [Minister] Montes de Oca." Legorreta was "not confident" that he would be successful.[41]

Lamont continued to pressure Montes de Oca to conclude the desired agreement as quickly as possible. By late January 1929 they were on the brink of such an accord.[42] Once again Morrow's influence caused a postponement. Lamont became exasperated with his friend. "It looks to me," he wrote Morgan, "as if the Ambassador had completely estopped further progress." Lamont was certain that the Committee would not stand idly by while Morrow was "perfecting his Government claims." The point had probably arrived where the Committee would have to "join issue on this matter promptly" unless some reassurance were received from Morrow which he deemed "unlikely."[43]

Lamont evidently had misconstrued Morrow's intentions in objecting to the agreement. The ambassador was not opposed to the accord because his primary responsibility was

---

[41] Anderson to Lamont, January 2, 1929, Lamont Papers.

[42] Lamont to Montes de Oca, January 25, 1929, Morrow Papers.

[43] Lamont to Morgan, March 2, 1929, Box 192, Lamont Papers.

to protect American claims. His opposition stemmed solely from the often expressed belief that the "Mexican Government should consider itself insolvent and impose upon itself the same obligations with reference to dealing with its creditors that a Court would impose upon an insolvent corporation." By "insolvent" Morrow meant that the current income of Mexico was insufficient to meet its "running expenses and at the same time those of its debts which are immediately due and payable." Morrow believed it was in the interest of all creditors that Mexico's available surplus should be divided among it creditors on "some equitable principle" rather than in a "wholly haphazard way."[44]

Lamont maintained that a nation could never be "insolvent" since it always had the taxing power. Morrow countered that a nation could reach the point where despite the taxing power it could not meet in full its obligations. He believed that Mexico had reached that juncture.[45]

The Escobar revolution, which erupted on March 3, 1929, rendered the entire debate academic, since it drained the Mexican treasury of monies earmarked for debt service and caused a delay in the negotiation with the International Committee. The revolution was an attempted coup d'état

---

[44]"Memorandum for Capt. McBride," March 19, 1929, Morrow Papers.

[45]Morrow to J. Reuben Clark, Jr., March 12, 1929, ibid.

which broke out in Vera Cruz and the northern Mexican
states. It was led by General José Gonzalo Escobar assisted by the governor of Sonora and the military commanders
in the states of Chihuahua, Oaxaca and Sonora.

The revolutionaries were Obregónists who refused to
recognize the authority of provisional President Emilio
Portes Gil. Portes Gil had been elected to that post by the
Mexican Congress in September 1928 in the wake of the assassination of Obregón and Calles' refusal to seek reelection.
Portes Gil had been Secretary of Interior under Calles and
was his choice to succeed him as president after the Obregón murder. It was expected that he would continue Calles'
policies.[46] The provisional president was sworn in on December 1, 1928.[47]

Although Portes Gil had a reputation as being an "extreme radical," Morrow was "very much impressed" with him
and concluded that he seemed like a "direct, straightforward
man." Morrow believed that Portes Gil's new responsibilities
would "sober him."[48] Rublee would later describe Portes Gil
as "not a remarkable man in any way, not a strong man, but
he was cooperative."[49]

---

[46] Morrow to Lamont, October 12, 1928, Box 192, Lamont Papers.

[47] Portes Gil served as provisional president until February 5, 1930

[48] Morrow to Lamont, October 12, 1928, Box 192, Lamont Papers.

[49] Rublee, "Reminiscences," 222.

Upon the outbreak of the revolution, former president Calles was appointed Secretary of War and assumed control of military operations against the insurgents. Within two weeks the revolt in Vera Cruz collapsed. At the battles of Jimenez and LaReforma the rebellion was crushed. The swiftness and success with which Calles had put down the revolution gained him recognition throughout Mexico as a soldier of the republic which facilitated his rise to jefe máximo.[50]

The cost of suppressing the rebellion forced Montes de Oca to declare, in mid-April 1929, that it was unlikely that an agreement could be concluded with the International Committee in 1929.[51] Neither the uprising nor this decision served to dissuade Lamont. To the contrary, soon after the defeat of the rebels, Lamont wrote to J.P. Morgan & Company from Paris that recent events in Mexico served to reaffirm his "reluctant belief" that they must proceed "as vigorously as possible despite the Ambassador's attitude."[52]

Significantly, in the first quarter of 1929, while the Lamont-Morrow debate was heating up, lame-duck Secretary of State Kellogg demonstrated a dramatic new burst of ini-

---

[50] Nicolson, **Dwight Morrow**, 344. A detailed, if highly subjective, account of the revolution and its suppression is in Emilio Portes Gil, Quince años de politica mexicana (2nd ed., Mexico City, 1941), 247-281.

[51] Turlington, **Mexico and Her Foreign Creditors**, 317.

[52] Lamont to J.P. Morgan & Company, May 3, 1929, Box 192, Lamont Papers.

tiative with regard to Latin America in general and Mexico in particular. Partially as a result of questions raised concerning the Monroe Doctrine during debates held in conjunction with the ratification of the Kellogg-Briand pact in 1928, Kellogg asked J. Reuben Clark to make a thorough study of the Monroe Doctrine, including everything that had ever been said concerning it by American officials.[53]

The Clark "Memorandum on the Monroe Doctrine," written in late 1928, concluded that the Roosevelt corollary was an unreasonable interpretation of the Monroe Doctrine which had been designed to defend the hemisphere from European intervention not for use against Latin America. The "Memorandum" stated that the Monroe Doctrine was not "an instrument of violence and oppression" but a "wholly effective guarantee" of Latin American "freedom, independence, and territorial integrity."[54] The Clark "Memorandum" repudiated the Roosevelt corollary and acknowledged that the Monroe Doctrine's "right" to keep European nations out of Latin America did not give the United States a corresponding "right" to intervene there.

The Clark "Memorandum" was not published until 1930.

---

[53]Clark had been on Morrow's staff until appointed Undersecretary of State on August 31, 1928.

[54]U.S. Senate, 71st Cong., 2nd Sess., Memorandum on the Monroe Doctrine, Prepared by J. Reuben Clark, Undersecretary of State (Washington, D.C., 1930).

Secretary of State Henry L. Stimson is frequently, though erroneously, given credit for the stance taken in the document.[55] President Franklin D. Roosevelt too won worldwide attention for his "Good Neighbor" policy toward Latin America built on the principles espoused by the Clark "Memorandum." Yet this vitally important document was requested by Kellogg and was submitted to him on December 17, 1928, during the last months of the Coolidge administration.[56] It was the natural culmination of the policies that the State Department had been working towards in the Kellogg-Olds-Clark years. In reality the seeds of the "Good Neighbor" policy were carefully planted by these top State Department officials during the Coolidge presidency.

The reasons why Coolidge and Kellogg have not received recognition for the new policy are many. Kellogg was a conservative and changed only slowly. To his credit he was willing to learn from the more open-minded men on whom he depended for policy formulation. Unfortunately, by the time he came to articulate the doctrine inherent in the Clark "Memorandum" it was too late for him to implement it.

---

[55] See for example, Elting E. Morison, *Turmoil and Tradition: A Study of the Life and Times of Henry L. Stimson* (New York, 1960), 258, and Foster Rhea Dulles, *America's Rise to World Power* (New York, 1954), 156.

[56] Ellis, *Frank B. Kellogg*, 101-103.

Kellogg did make a valiant attempt to put the nonintervention policy into effect before he left the Department. On February 28, 1929, he wrote a note based on the memorandum which he intended to have distributed to American representatives throughout Latin America for delivery to the governments to which they were assigned. The note stated that the Monroe Doctrine was not an instrument of "hostility or aggression or an intent to control or direct the affairs of Latin American States by the United States." Kellogg further declared that "The Monroe Doctrine is not now and never was an instrument of aggression; it is and always has been a cloak of protection. The Doctrine is not a lance; it is a shield."[57]

In his last days at the State Department, Kellog consulted with Stimson as to his opinion regarding the wisdom of the note and apparently believed that the incoming Secretary approved. Kellogg therefore sent the note to American representatives throughout Latin America with orders that they await further instructions before presenting the notes to the governments concerned. Kellogg assumed that such instructions soon would be forthcoming under Stimson but the latter apparently was hesitant to take the bold step.[58]

---

[57] Kellogg Memorandum, February 28, 1929, FRUS 1929, I, 698-719.

[58] Ellis, Frank B. Kellogg, 103-104. The Kellogg note was neither delivered nor published until 1943.

The Clark "Memorandum" and the Kellogg note are significant for Mexico. Under the rules of international law existing in 1929, governments were entitled to intervene in behalf of their nationals "for the purpose of enforcing the performance of justice to its citizens" when a "foreign State has become itself the debtor of these citizens."[59] The United States, by virtue of the 1907 Hague Convention, had agreed not to intervene unless it could not persuade the debtor nation to submit to arbitration.[60] Thus there was always the possibility that the United States would intervene in Mexico to obtain justice for its citizens who were Mexico's creditors. The Kellogg note was a formal disavowal of such intentions.

On his last day as Secretary of State, Kellogg sent lengthy and detailed instructions to Morrow as to how he should respond to the various problems that continued to plague him in Mexico. Kellogg took his most forthright stand on the question of Mexico's debts. Morrow was ordered to oppose vigorously any new agreement between the Mexican government and any individual group of creditors. Kellogg's comments were clearly directed at the International Committee.[61]

---

[59] Turlington, Mexico and Her Foreign Creditors, 321 fn.

[60] James B. Scott, The Hague Convention and Declarations of 1899 and 1907 (New York, 1915), 236.

[61] Kellogg to Morrow, March 27, 1929, Morrow Papers.

Kellogg provided Morrow with a long history of the treatment under civil law of claims against an insolvent. He emphasized the fact that secured claims did not necessarily get priority. Morrow was directed to inform the Mexican government that the United States "must ask and will expect that all American creditors...will be treated on an equivalent basis so far as preferences and priorities are concerned." Bondholders, Kellogg maintained, can "hardly be placed higher than other claimants who have been tortiously deprived of their property or property rights." Although the Department did not believe it necessary now to insist upon strict preferences and priorities, it might in the future be forced to do so should the bondholders follow a course which necessitated that other American claimants be protected.[62] Morrow, of course, was in total agreement with the policy outlined by Kellogg. The Escobar revolution made it unnecessary for him to press the issue for the time being.

Since, temporarily, he did not need to devote his time and energies to fighting an agreement between the International Committee and Mexico, Morrow was able to tackle the church-state problem once again. He had succeeded in winning the respect of President Portes Gil who called him "<u>personal amigo mío</u>."[63] Having established this rapport, Morrow was able

---

[62]<u>Ibid</u>.

[63]Portes Gil, <u>Quince anos</u>, 318.

to move Portes Gil and the Catholic Church toward an understanding. The Mexican described Morrow as a "humane diplomat," one who desired "to serve his nation without provoking hatred for northamerican power."[64]

In early May 1929, Portes Gil indicated in an interview with a New York newspaper that he was prepared to compromise with the church. Archbishop Leopoldo Ruiz y Flores, the apostolic delegate, responded favorably on behalf of the church. With Morrow functioning as mediator, Portes Gil and Archbishop Ruiz were able quickly to conclude an agreement on June 19, 1929, which proved acceptable both to the Vatican and to Mexico.[65]

It was agreed that the Church would resume its religious functions. The government declared that it had no intention of destroying the identity of the Church. Priests must continue to register in accordance with the Constitution but they would be appointed by the religious hierarchy. Religious instruction once again could be given in churches but not in schools. Catholics could petition Congress for amendments to objectionable constitutional provisions.[66] This agreement brought an end to the longstanding controversy which had caused bloodshed and cost Mexico inestimable

---

[64] Ibid., 357.

[65] Nicolson, Dwight Morrow, 345-346.

[66] Portes Gil, Quince años, 306-318.

pesos. Both sides credited Morrow with functioning as the catalyst for peace.

Unfortunately all Morrow's efforts were not so successful. The friction with Lamont and the International Committee continued, with Lamont singlemindedly pursuing the elusive agreement with Mexico on behalf of the bondholders the Committee represented. Morrow continued to oppose it both in his talks with Mexican leaders and in his correspondence with the Committee.[67]

Morrow had received assurances through the new Undersecretary of State, Joseph P. Cotton,[68] his friend since 1901, that "neither he [Cotton] nor Stimson would specifically concern themselves" with Mexico. They would leave it to Morrow to "do whatever you thought best." The only proviso was that they be kept informed "so that no action there would take the Secretary or President by surprise."[69]

With this support from the State Department and with the firm backing of his French and English counterparts in Mexico City, Ministers Jean Perier and Sir Esmond Ovey, Morrow continued to press for a comprehensive agreement.[70] While in New York, in late August 1929, Morrow discussed

---

[67]See Morrow to Munroe, July 10, 1929, Morrow Papers.
[68]Cotton was confirmed in the position on June 8, 1929.
[69]Rublee to Morrow, July 18, 1929, Morrow Papers.
[70]Jean Perier to Sir Esmond Ovey, August 16, 1929, ibid.

the issue with Anderson and concluded that the Committee was perhaps "more encouraged than they should be" about Mexico. In these talks Morrow emphasized the necessity of making an "absolute division" of the funds available to be applied to the debt in 1930.[71]

On October 2, 1929, the differences of opinion between the Department and the Committee were discussed at length in a top level conference held at the State Department. Among those present were Secretary Stimson, Undersecretary Cotton, Morrow, Lamont and McBride. Morrow suggested that there were three alternatives that could be followed with regard to Mexico's debts. The International Committee could take the lead in forming a larger Committee to include all important classes of creditors. This committee could prepare an "omnibus plan" for the settlement of the entire Mexican debt. Alternatively, the Mexican and/or United States governments could initiate the organization of such a committee. Or thirdly, the current approach could be continued with partial settlements being concluded in a haphazard manner without consideration for the relative rights of the various creditors.[72]

The Committee representatives responded that they could

---

[71] Morrow to McBride, August 30, 1929, ibid.

[72] Minutes of conference held October 2, 1929, taken by Munroe, dated October 3, 1929, Box 196, Lamont Papers.

not take the lead in forming a larger committee but would
cooperate if one or both of the governments took such initiative. Cotton intimated that the United States could not
participate in the formation of such a committee. Stimson
expressed the hope that some way could be found to "unite
on some plan." But he cautioned the Committee that if this
were not possible, the State Department would have no obligation to it whatsoever. To the contrary, there would be a
clear obligation to support other claims against the Mexican government that seemed to have "greater weight" even
than those of the bondholders. This, the Secretary indicated, did not mean that the Department was in opposition to
the Committee but would be in "competition" with it. He hinted that the Department would be in a position to assert
greater influence on the Mexican government than the Committee could.[73]

Stimson stated that the United States felt a duty to
the government of Mexico as well as to the claimants. Lamont contended that the Commitee's policy had always been
one of "consideration for Mexico in her difficulties, acknowledgement of the obligations of Mexico to other than the
Committee, and always one of helpfulness for Mexico to ease
her over her troubles." It was agreed that the State Depart-

---

[73]Ibid.

ment and Committee would cooperate to influence the Mexican government in the disposition of its 1930 surplus, if any.[74]

Throughout the month of October 1929 McBride and Rublee met in New York with members of the Committee in an attempt to arrive at an agreement as to how Mexico's surplus for 1930 could best be divided. Both men continually emphasized the need for one, comprehensive plan. McBride stressed the futility of separate agreements. He pointed out that this approach placed the burden on the Minister of Finance to determine priorities. He could not handle this objectively because he was "subject to great pressure from interested parties."[75]

The Committee expressed its willingness to cooperate but favored a separate agreement on the bonded debt. They were willing to see it as a part of a general arrangement covering the entire debt.[76] The extent of the breach between Morrow and Lamont was evidenced by Lamont's comments to Cotton that the ambassador was "considerably fooled by the Mexicans." Lamont found Morrow to be "just as nice as

---

[74] Ibid.

[75] Memorandum of talks in New York with representatives of International Committee of Bankers on Mexico, October 7-9, 1929, Morrow Papers; Rublee to Morrow, October 11, 1929, ibid.

[76] "Memorandum of Telephone Conversation with Mr. Anderson," October 22, 1929, written by McBride, ibid.

he was but...his plans are terribly vague." Lamont felt that Morrow was so fond of individuals in Mexico that he was easily deceived by them.[77]

Once again Lamont had underestimated his friend. Morrow understood the real disagreement was not over whether Mexico was insolvent but rather whether that insolvency was an "honest one." The Committee, he felt, thought that Mexico would have more funds available if "she would mend her ways." He agreed that there would be "*more* of a surplus to divide amongst creditors if public affairs were conducted in a different way." But always the pragmatist, Morrow viewed the problem in terms of what should be done with the surplus which actually was available.[78]

Morrow attempted to increase the surplus available. One of the chief drains on the Mexican treasury long had been the agrarian reform program. Portes Gil was a firm advocate of land reform. He accelerated the program during his short term as president. The more conservative Calles and Minister Montes de Oca had urged him to pay cash for the land. Portes Gil refused. The cash available would be inadequate, he maintained, and it would be politically unpopular in an election year.[79]

---

[77] "Memorandum of Telephone Conversation with Thomas W. Lamont," October 18, 1929, written by Cotton, ibid.

[78] Morrow to Green H. Hackworth, October 29, 1929, ibid.

[79] Portes Gil, Quince anos, 52-53.

During the 1929 presidential campaign, Pascual Ortiz Rubio, candidate of the new official party--Partido Nacional Revolucionario--gave speeches hinting at a more conservative land reform policy, even promising to pay cash for land. Calles went so far as to say that agrarian reform had failed, had sapped the nation's finances, and must be terminated. Reflecting this position on the part of his party, Portes Gil took steps which effectively restricted land reform.[80] Morrow had been instrumental in convincing Calles over a two year period that the land reform policy, as then constituted, was not in the best interests of Mexico. Calles' opinion was quickly adopted by those who owed their political careers to him.

In November 1929 Morrow's diplomatic and political horizons were unexpectedly broadened. On November 12, Stimson asked him to serve on the American delegation to the London Naval Conference. Morrow accepted.[81] Two weeks later, Morrow was asked to accept the senate seat from New Jersey which had become vacant when Senator Walter E. Edge was appointed Ambassador to Paris. These conflicting opportunities provided a temporary dilemma which was quickly resolved when a stand-in was appointed senator until Morrow became available

---

[80] Stanley R. Ross, "Dwight Morrow and the Mexican Revolution," *Hispanic American Historical Review*, XXXVIII (November 1958), 522-523.

[81] In late 1928 and early 1929 rumors abounded that Morrow would be appointed Secretary of State in the Hoover cabinet. Hoover discussed the post with Morrow and the ambassador indicated that he had not yet completed his task in Mexico. Nicolson, *Dwight Morrow*, 348-350.

after the London Conference. Morrow was aware that his influence and success in Mexico could not endure indefinitely and responded to the urgings of family and friends to try his hand at politics.[82] He left Mexico for London on January 9, 1930, and did not return to the embassy until July 3 of that year.

---

[82] *Ibid.*, 350-353.

CHAPTER VI

MORROW VERSUS LAMONT

Morrow returned to the embassy in Mexico City on July 3, 1930, almost six months after he had departed for London. While he had been representing the United States at the naval conference (until late April) and engaging in the successful primary campaign for the Republican senate nomination from New Jersey, important changes had occurred in Mexico. Ortiz Rubio had become president on February 5, 1930. In the absence of the forceful, persuasive ambassador, the new president and Finance Minister Montes de Oca were vulnerable to pressures from the International Committee.

Morrow was handicapped on his return because the Mexicans knew that he would only be in Mexico a few more months. They could not be sure of policy continuity. Morrow was further impeded by an indiscreet speech made on his behalf in the New Jersey campaign by his former military attaché, Colonel Alexander Macnab. In his enthusiasm for Morrow's candidacy, Macnab credited the ambassador with having put Mexico "on her feet." Even more damaging, in view of Mexican sensitivities, Macnab declared that, "There is no department of government in Mexico which he [Morrow] had not advised and directed. He took the Secretary of Finance under his wing and taught him finance."[1]

---

[1]Nicolson, *Dwight Morrow*, 382.

This imprudent speech did not reflect Morrow's role accurately and certainly had not had his blessing. Macnab retracted his statements but the damage was done. Montes de Oca, who considered himself a friend of Morrow and who had been "very useful" to the ambassador, was deeply offended by the implication that he had been spoon fed by Morrow. The new president, who knew Morrow less well than did Montes de Oca, and the entire Mexican cabinet were cool towards the ambassador. Much of the goodwill he had built up over the past 30 months had been dissipated in a single speech.[2]

The timing of this embarrassment was particularly unfortunate in that Montes de Oca was then preparing for a trip to New York upon Lamont's invitation to discuss a new plan for the settlement of the external debt questions. In late 1929, before Morrow left Mexico for London, he and Lamont had worked rather closely once again.[3] Both men hoped that the Ortiz Rubio administration could be influenced to allocate a larger portion of its 1930 budget for debt service. It is not likely that Lamont was convinced that one comprehensive plan was a desirable goal. Yet it was in the Committee's interest that he cooperate in any attempt to increase the amount available for debt service. Morrow was

---

[2] Rublee, "Reminiscences," 225-226.

[3] Morrow to Cotton, November 8, 1929, Morrow Papers.

advocating an increase of about 13 million pesos. This figure would be raised by reducing other expenditures.[4]

Morrow had been optimistic that the new administration could be moved in this direction. His friend, Calles, was in agreement that a "larger amount" should be made available for application to Mexico's debts. Calles was expected to wield greater influence with the new president, who owed his position to the former executive. Ortiz Rubio had gone so far as to state that it was a "wonderful thing" for Mexico to have a former president with the "character and wisdom of Calles available for consultation." He also felt that all future Mexican presidents were "bound to seek his advice and guidance" so long as he lived.[5]

Just prior to leaving for London Morrow once again stressed in his report to Stimson for 1929 that,

> The Government in justice to its creditors should adopt a method of apportioning whatever annual surplus is applicable to debt amongst the various classes of creditors according to just and equitable principles rather than in the arbitrary manner that has prevailed in the past.[6]

Morrow steadfastly clung to his belief that no partial settlement could be of permanent benefit. Although the Mexican government in 1930 regularly pressed Morrow to conclude an en bloc settlement of the claims against it by American cit-

---

[4] "Memorandum to T.W. Lamont," December 11, 1929, written by Munroe, Box 192, Lamont Papers.

[5] Morrow to Clark, December 16, 1929, Morrow Papers.

[6] Morrow to Stimson, December 31, 1929, ibid.

izens,[7] Morrow refused since he believed that a separate agreement regarding claims was of no more value than the kinds of agreements the International Committee futilely had concluded. He was unwilling "to sacrifice what he considered a simple fundamental principle for any temporary advantage." He remained firm in this view despite contrary advice from some of his most trusted advisers and autorization from the State Department to engage in negotiations for such an *en bloc* settlement.[8]

Morrow wrote Ortiz Rubio just three days before departing for London that "the most important task" of his administration was to work out a settlement that would "do equity and justice to the various groups of creditors who have claims against Mexico."[9] Morrow apparently was confident that Lamont would continue to cooperate. Lamont encouraged him in this belief.[10]

While Morrow was occupied in London, Lamont and his associates applied heavy pressure on the new Mexican administration to conclude a separate agreement with the Commit-

---

[7] See Morrow to Stimson, July 16, 1930, August 7, 1930, and September 4, 1930, all in FRUS 1930, III, 495-498.

[8] McBride to Nicolson, June 24, 1935, Private Papers of Captain Lewis B. McBride in the possession of Mrs. Lewis B. McBride, Washington, D.C. (Hereafter cited as McBride Papers.); Stimson to Morrow, July 17, 1930, FRUS 1930, III, 496.

[9] Morrow to Ortiz Rubio, January 6, 1930, Morrow Papers.

[10] Lamont to Morrow, January 17, 1930, ibid.

tee. This action should not be attributed to mere duplicity on Lamont's part. Lamont was aware that Morrow would soon be giving up his post in exchange for a political career. It could not be known how cooperative his successor would be. Additionally, Lamont was himself under pressure from the European sections of the Committee to reach some type of accord with the Mexicans. Lamont came to believe that further delay, particularly in view of Morrow's imminent departure from Mexico, would compromise his leadership position with the Committee and potentially could result in its fragmentation into separate, competing groups on a nation by nation basis.[11]

The Macnab indiscretion played into Lamont's hands. There were enough ruffled feathers in Mexico to gain Lamont success in inducing the administration to hold new discussions. The Mexicans were determined to demonstrate their independence from Morrow's "guidance."[12]

---

[11] Charles F. Whigham to Lamont, February 16, 1929; Lamont to J. Ridgely Carter for Jacques Kulp, July 7, 1930; Lamont to Carter, August 22, 1930; Lamont to Morrow, July 24, 1930, all in Box 192, Lamont Papers; Morrow to McBride, February 10, 1930, Morrow Papers.

[12] Nicolson, Dwight Morrow, 382-383. The section in Nicolson on the debt question was edited by McBride "to give a truer picture" of Morrow's policy. McBride was still not totally satisfied with the finished product but Nicolson used it nonetheless, with only two insignificant changes. Rublee was dissatisfied with Nicolson's portrayal of Morrow's years in Mexico. Still, he believed that McBride had done all he possibly could to make it more accurate. McBride to Rublee, May 7, 1935; Rublee to McBride, May 9, 1935; Nicolson to McBride, May 30, 1935; McBride to Nicolson, June 24, 1935; all in McBride Papers. Rublee, "Reminiscences," 200-201.

In late June 1930 Montes de Oca went to New York to begin discussions. Lamont intended to take advantage of the political stability which resulted in part from American policy of support "against unwarranted revolution" as well as from the conservative economic policies Montes de Oca had instituted in order to conclude a "firm and permanent" agreement. He believed that the conditions were then more favorable to such an accord than they had ever been before.[13]

There was little Morrow could do to prevent the agreement from being concluded. Lamont telephoned him on July 10, 1930, to inform him of the progress of the negotiations. Morrow indicated that merely reducing the amount of Mexico's debt to the Committee would not guarantee an enduring accord unless all other creditors also reduced their claims. To the contrary, other creditors would probably view an agreement with the Committee as an indication that they would be paid in full. Lamont disagreed.[14]

McBride expressed to Sterrett Morrow's concern that the agreement under discussion would not constitute "a safe and conservative contribution to the reestablishment of Mexican credit." Only a comprehensive plan would be in the interest of all creditors.[15]

---

[13] Lamont to Carter, July 7, 1930, Box 192, Lamont Papers.
[14] Memorandum by Morrow, July 10, 1930, Morrow Papers.
[15] McBride to Sterrett, July 16, 1930, ibid.

In a final desperate attempt to prevent the signing of an agreement, Morrow telephoned Lamont from Mexico. Lamont admitted that the agreement under discussion would not be conditioned on any other agreements with other classes of creditors. He responded to Morrow's expressions of disappointment and concern by stating that it was his undertanding that Montes de Oca felt that if he made an agreement with the Committee with regard to the bonded debt he could still "make suitable provision for other classes of creditors." Morrow "reminded" Lamont that this was a "natural position for an inexperienced insolvent debtor to take." The debtor would conclude separate agreements with "arbitrary concessions" and "new promises" without satisfactory provisions for fulfilling them. The result was that the debtor remained insolvent. Morrow suggested that the proposed agreement be postponed for at least a year.[16]

Lamont obviously was upset by the rigid stance of his good friend, particularly since an agreement awaited only the final signatures. On July 24, 1930, he wrote Morrow a lengthy letter in which he expressed sadness that they could not agree and hoped that Morrow would not oppose ratification of the agreement which he implied was already drawn up. Lamont emphasized that it was Montes de Oca who insisted

---

[16] Memorandum of phone conversation between Lamont and Morrow, July 23, 1930, ibid.

that the accord be concluded immediately as the initial step towards the resolution of Mexico's complex financial problems. The Mexican Minister had stipulated that the agreement could not "impair his ability to make a reasonably satisfactory settlement" of Mexico's other debts. Montes de Oca reportedly maintained that the pressures from foreign bondholders other than the Committee were so great that to postpone the agreement any longer would cost the Committee its membership and make his job that much more difficult.[17]

Morrow maintained that it would be immoral for the Committee to become a signatory to an agreement calling for a reduction in the funds due the bondholders it represented, since such an accord was doomed to almost certain failure (judging from the history of Mexican defaults on all previous agreements). Lamont disagreed strongly. He shared the view of Montes de Oca that the earlier agreements had broken down as the direct result of revolutions. Barring a new rebellion, the accord being contemplated was "so well within Mexico's capacity to pay...that it should be fulfilled."[18]

Morrow had made a thinly veiled threat that the State Department "would be likely to make a protest to the Mexican Government and try to prevent the settlement from going

---

[17] Lamont to Morrow, July 24, 1930, Box 192, Lamont Papers.

[18] Ibid.

through." Lamont expressed doubt that the Department would be willing to antagonize foreign nationals who had been waiting so long to collect from Mexico by opposing an agreement with a Mexican government that was willing and able to pay.[19]

Lamont stated his hope that in view of the circumstances Morrow could see his way clear to "letting the matter rest where it is rather than feeling called upon to attempt to defeat the plan." It seemed particularly important to Lamont that Morrow not oppose the accord since it was favored by both Ortiz Rubio and Montes de Oca. Lamont argued that a defeat by the Mexican Congress would be a "black eye for Mexican prestige." Opposition to the pact might prove to be a "grave disservice to Mexico."[20]

The next day, July 25, 1930, Morrow received a telegram informing him that the agreement had been signed that afternoon. Lamont expressed hope that "you will not take me too severely to task."[21]

The Lamont-Montes de Oca agreement called for the exchange of the various issues comprising Mexico's direct debt for new 45-year bonds secured against the entire customs revenues. The new bonds would be issued in series A and B.

---

[19] Ibid.

[20] Ibid.

[21] Lamont to Morrow, July 25, 1930, Morrow Papers.

Both series initially would carry an interest rate of three percent, graduated annually to five percent for the series A in 1935 and in 1936 for the series B. The Mexican government would pay annuities to cover the service on the new debt to the Committee, beginning with $12.5 million in 1931 and increasing annually to $15 million in 1936 and thereafter. Out of the first five annuity payments would come a fund of $11.75 million to be applied to the full liquidation of interest arrears. The agreement also included a memorandum outlining an arrangement to be concluded in a separate agreement between the National Railways of Mexico and its bondholders.[22]

In his opposition to the Lamont-Montes de Oca agreement Morrow enjoyed the full support of the State Department. In the absence of Stimson, who spent his summers in virtual seclusion in the Maine woods, Cotton handled the Mexican questions. He expressed the opinion to Lamont that the accord was "premature." He informed Morrow that Lamont's response was one of "pained surprise." Cotton believed the settlement to be "too ambitious." He felt the agreement was based on Lamont's belief that Mexico could pay if it wanted to. Therefore, Lamont pursued "new promises," which Cotton felt were not of "substantial value unless a part of a

---

[22] Statement by the International Committee of Bankers on Mexico, dated July 25, 1930, and Letter from International Committee to Bondholders, signed by Munroe, August 30, 1930, both in Box 192, Lamont Papers.

general scheme." The difficulty, in the immediate future, with any general scheme was that "Mexico has its domestic house to put in order."[23]

Cotton stated in a memorandum written to Morrow on August 3, 1930, that the attitude of the Department towards the new agreement would be "determined by the Department--not by the Ambassador." Yet he indicated that he would like the "full comments" of the ambassador regarding his views and the conclusions he drew.[24] It is most likely that this statement was intended merely for the record and in anticipation of complaints from the International Committee that the tail was wagging the dog. There can be no question that the Department was asserting its authority over the issue primarily because Morrow's departure was only weeks away and a new ambassador had not yet been named to succeed him. Policy continuity could be provided by having the Department in direct control of decisions made regarding the new pact. Morrow understood this to be the case and was in complete agreement.

Cotton took care to mention in the memorandum that Lamont had not asked the consent of the Department to the agreement because he viewed it as a private arrangement. Had he asked the Department, Cotton indicated, he would

---

[23] Cotton to Morrow, July 29, 1930, Morrow Papers.

[24] "Memorandum on Mexican Debt," August 3, 1930, written by Cotton, *ibid.*

have been told that "such a separate agreement is not much value to him and foolish for Mexico." Cotton wondered if Montes de Oca's expressed intention to adjust Mexico's other debts was "anything more than a wish."[25]

The undersecretary went on to enumerate his objections to the accord. He denied the right of the Internatioanl Committee to all the customs revenues, since this was such an important source of Mexico's income. He stated that he was not willing to "stand mute" while any group of creditors received exclusive rights to an important source of revenue. He contemplated that the Department would inform Mexico that even if the agreement was ratified, the United States would not regard it as binding. He expressed doubt as to whether the various state bonds covered by the agreement were actually debts of the Mexican government. He believed that the initial payment to be made by Mexico was unrealistically high. Cotton further asserted that the agreement might be in violation of legal priorities, once the United States asserted them. Lastly, he doubted the wisdom of the provision for future loans. Ultimately the Department's position on the agreement would be determined by whether or not Mexico actually initiated active negotiations with regard to other obligations.[26]

---

[25] Ibid.
[26] Ibid.

Morrow responded to the Cotton memorandum by indicating his firm belief that the agreement if ratified "independently of a general project with budgetary provisions therefor" would be unwise for Mexico and for "its creditors including the bondholders represented by the International Committee." He recommended, however, that the Department take no steps in opposition to the agreement "until the matter had proceeded further," except "so far as necessary to protect American interests for which the State Department is under responsibility." This was consistent with the traditional stance of the Department that it was "too great a responsibility to advise them [the Mexicans] not to pay creditors."[27]

On August 15, 1930, a presidential *acuerdo colectivo* approved the Lamont-Montes de Oca agreement. Morrow, however, was doing all in his power to convince the Mexican leaders that ratification of the agreement would be a grave mistake. In private discussions on August 20 with President Ortiz Rubio and Foreign Minister Genero Estrada, Morrow stressed time and again that Mexico must formulate a "general project" before ratification of the Lamont-Montes de Oca pact.[28] He furnished Ortiz Rubio with a letter expressing his views and a memorandum prepared by McBride which pointed out the pitfalls of the new accord and discussed the general reor-

---

[27] Morrow to Stimson, August 21, 1930, FRUS 1930, III, 475-477.

[28] Ibid.

ganization of the entire Mexican debt. McBride argued that the agreement was a violation of Montes de Oca's own policies and a "repetition of previous errors." He suggested that the Lamont-Montes de Oca agreement be submitted to Congress in 1930 as part of a comprehensive plan. He believed that Montes de Oca was capable of formulating such a plan.[29]

Ortiz Rubio agreed not to submit the Lamont-Montes de Oca agreement to the Mexican Congress except as part of a general plan.[30] It was Morrow's friendship with Foreign Minister Estrada which made this concession possible.[31] In the absence of Montes de Oca, who was still in New York, Estrada helped Morrow convince Ortiz Rubio that this action was in Mexico's best interests. When Montes de Oca returned to Mexico he was enraged to learn that the president had made this commitment and that the Morrow letter made the ambassador's influence a matter of record. Ortiz Rubio was compelled to ask Morrow to withdraw his letter in interest of harmony within his cabinet. This did not alter, however, the president's commitment; nor was McBride's memorandum withdrawn.[32]

---

[29] Memorandum for Ambassador Morrow, August 22, 1930, written by McBride, Morrow Papers.

[30] McBride to Nicolson, June 24, 1935, McBride Papers; Morrow to State Department, August 21, 1930, Morrow Papers.

[31] Nicolson, *Dwight Morrow*, 336.

[32] McBride to Nicolson, June 24, 1935, McBride Papers.

Morrow informed Lamont that unfortunately their differences were more than "philosophical" as the latter had suggested. They were in fact the result of a fundamental "difference in our understanding of the facts." Morrow believed that the Mexican government "is now, and has been for several years, insolvent." "This," he maintained, "is not a theory but a fact." Morrow called Lamont's attention to the Egyptian precedent. He declared that the condition of insolvency placed certain duties on the Mexican government with regard to its creditors and on the creditors with regard to each other. He implied that the controversial agreement was in violation of those duties. Morrow was still hopeful that the agreement could be incorporated in a comprehensive plan. If it were not, however, and ratification of the accord was proposed without any provision for other creditors, the State Department, as Cotton had stated, would determine what steps it should take for the security of American interests. The threat of formal State Department opposition was clear.[33]

Less than a month later, on September 17, 1930, Morrow departed from Mexico permanently to prepare for the November senatorial election, which he would win easily. With his major opponent out of the way, Lamont turned his guns

---

[33] Morrow to Lamont, August 18, 1930, Box 192, Lamont Papers.

on the State Department, barraging it with argument upon
argument as to why it should not oppose the ratification
of the agreement. He complained to Cotton that the Egyptian precedent that Morrow and McBride had relied upon was
not analagous to the Mexican situation. He claimed that if
Morrow would be available to "administer Mexican Government
finances for the next ten years" the Committee would be willing to do things his way. But, alas, that would not be the
case.[34]

Lamont had no success in obtaining State Department
sanction for the agreement. The Hoover-Stimson administration was determined to continue in the direction begun under Coolidge and Kellogg. In his pre-inaugural good-will
tour of Latin America, Hoover had assured his hosts that
the United States desired "to maintain not only the cordial
relations of governments with each other but the relations
of good neighbors." In Montevideo Hoover expressed the hope
that "I might by this visit symbolize the courtesy of a
call from one good neighbor to another, that I might convey
the respect, esteem, and desire for intellectual and spiritual cooperation.[35]

---

[34] Morrow to Lamont, August 18, 1930, Box 192, Lamont Papers.

[35] Addresses Delivered During the Visit of Herbert Hoover, President-elect of the United States, to Central and South America, November-December 1928 (Washington, D.C., 1929), 36. See Alexander DeConde, Herbert Hoover's Latin American Policy (New York, 1951), ch. 2, for full discussion of the significance of Hoover's Latin American tour.

In his inaugural address Hoover signaled the direction his foreign policy would take when he stated that "we have no desire for territorial expansion, for economic or other domination of other people. Such purposes are repugnant to our ideals of human freedom.... We wish to advance the reign of justice and reason toward the extinction of force."[36] In 1930 Hoover formally embraced a non-intervention policy towards Latin America and caused the Clark "Memorandum" to be published.[37]

Hoover and Stimson were determined to make United States policy towards Latin America "so clear in its implications of justice and goodwill, in its avoidance of anything which could be even misconstrued into a policy of forceful intervention or desire for exploitation of those republics and their citizens, as to reassure the most timid or suspicious among them."[38] As part of this approach to Latin America, Stimson refused to use "the authority and weight of the American Government on behalf of the financial interests of pri-

---

[36] U.S. Senate, 71st Cong., Special Session, *Inaugural Address by President Herbert Hoover, March 4, 1929* (Washington, D.C., 1929).

[37] DeConde, *Hoover's Latin American Policy*, 49.

[38] Henry L. Stimson, "Bases of American Foreign Policy During the Past Four Years," *Foreign Affairs*, XI (April 1933), 394-395.

vate citizens in Latin America."[39]

Stimson responded to pressure from Lamont with a reminder that the Lamont-Montes de Oca agreement had not been submitted to the Department for consideration, and although the Department was not asserting that consultation should have occurred, it would not want its silence to be misunderstood as approval of the accord. To the contrary, the Department had serious reservations with regard to some facets of the agreement. For example, the new accord decreased the total face amount of the debt but increased the aggregate amount of secured bonds represented by the Committee. Should the agreement "impair the resources available for meeting the balance of Mexican foreign debt" either because of its claims on revenues or because it necessitated that an "unfair share" of Mexico's national resources were applied to the foreign debt, the Department would feel free "to disregard" the terms of the agreement.[40] The Mexican ambassador was sent a copy of Stimson's letter to Lamont informing him of the Department's position.

The Mexican government had complied with the agreement's stipulation that it deposit $5 million with the Committee on account of the first annuity, that amount to be held pending ratification of the accord. Still, Ortiz Rubio's second

---

[39] Henry L. Stimson and McGeorge Bundy, On Active Service in Peace and War (New York, 1947), 181.

[40] Stimson to Lamont, October 6, 1930, FRUS 1930, III, 490-492.

thoughts on the matter jeopardized ratification. The Mexican president delayed sending the agreement to Congress and then requested that the senators and deputies "study the question painstakingly since there may have been error on the part of the Executive" in concluding the agreement. He asked that the Congress "carefully analyze the legal, political and economic aspects" of the pact.[41]

The worldwide depression precipitated a political and economic crisis in Mexico. Revenues declined sharply. Four representatives from the state of Chihuahua introduced a bill in the Chamber of Deputies calling for a ten-year moratorium on the foreign debt. Many senators attacked Montes de Oca for negotiating the accord secretly without consulting Congress. The pique of the Mexican Congress and the mushrooming depression ensured that the session would end on December 31 without the pact being ratified.[42] Seeing the handwriting on the wall, Montes de Oca initiated correspondence with the Committee aimed at some modifications of the accord which might render it more acceptable to congress.[43]

Meanwhile, on October 3, 1930, Hoover had appointed a new ambassador to Mexico, J. Reuben Clark Jr., who had extensive diplomatic experience both in Mexico City and in the

---

[41] Arthur Bliss Lane to Stimson, October 21, 1930, ibid., 492; McBride to Morrow, October 10, 1930 and October 31, 1930, Morrow Papers.

[42] McBride to Morrow, December 22, 1930, ibid.

[43] Clark to Stimson, December 2, 1930, FRUS 1930, III, 493-494.

State Department, was a logical successor to Morrow. In late 1927 and early 1928 Clark had served on Morrow's personal staff at the embassy, advising the ambassador on the oil controversy. From September 1928 until March 1929, Clark was Undersecretary of State. In that position he had written the famous "Memorandum on the Monroe Doctrine," which became the cornerstone of Franklin Roosevelt's "good neighbor" policy.[44] It rejected intervention as an instrument of American diplomacy in Latin America. Clark was well-suited to continue the State Department policies that he had helped formulate.

As the impact of the depression on Mexico became more severe, popular opposition to the Lamont-Montes de Oca agreement intensified. Many Mexicans considered the International Committee and Wall Street as synonymous. The depression was viewed simplistically by many Mexicans as having been caused by New York bankers. Montes de Oca was attacked as a "tool of Wall Street."[45] The Committee was charged with being a Shylock in pursuit of its pound of flesh.[46]

---

[44] DeConde, Hoover's Latin American Policy, 49. Dana Munro, The United States and the Caribbean Republics, 375-379, denies that the Clark Memorandum represented a change in policy towards Latin America.

[45] Clark to Stimson, December 2, 1930, FRUS 1930, III, 493-494.

[46] Memorandum for Lamont, November 29, 1930, Box 192, Lamont Papers.

The agreement looked particularly undesirable in view of an approximately four-fold increase in the discount on silver pesos as against the gold pesos between July and December 1920. (The bulk of the nation's revenues were collected in silver.) The current exchange and discount rates would bring Mexico's loss on the $7.5 million in gold dollars due the Committee toward the 1931 payments to approximately $2.5 million.[47]

In view of the deteriorating conditions, Montes de Oca proposed to Lamont that the agreement they had concluded on July 25, 1930, be modified to facilitate ratification. He suggested two alternative proposals. One, that the balance due on account of 1931 payments be deposited in silver at the current rate of exchange in any bank in Mexico City designated by the Committee, thus reducing the amount of silver in circulation and hopefully its value in relation to gold. Under any circumstances, he indicated, the gold reserves were insufficient to allow payment of the $7.5 million in that metal. The second alternative was simply to ratify the agreement, but that its effective date be postponed one year, to January 1, 1932.[48]

Lamont immediately recognized that the agreement could

---

[47] Clark to Stimson, December 2, 1930, FRUS 1930, III, 493-494.

[48] Ibid., 494-495.

not be honored as it stood. He conceded to Montes de Oca's suggested alternatives with minor changes. On January 29, 1931, a supplementary accord was signed which suspended transfers for two years, although the payments due under the agreement would continue to be made in silver to a Mexico City bank. The exchange rate for silver was fixed at 45.25 United States cents per silver peso, the prevailing rate on July 25, 1930. The accumulated deposits would be remitted to New York whenever the silver peso again returned to its July 25, 1925, value.[49]

The depression had made it unnecessary for the State Department or Ambassador Clark to oppose actively the Lamont-Montes de Oca agreement. For all practical purposes it was a dead issue. By May 1931 the average monthly discount rate on the silver peso was 25.2 percent. On July 25, 1931, it reached 36 percent. One year earlier the discount rate had been only 4.5 percent. There was no prospect for a reversal in the forseeable future.[50]

In response to the plight of the silver peso, a new monetary law was enacted on June 25, 1931. This law demonetarized gold and placed Mexico on a silver standard. Called the Plan Calles, although it was formulated by Montes de Oca, the new legislation made the silver peso legal tender

---

[49]Clark to Stimson, December 27, 1930, ibid., 495; Wynne, State Insolvency, 82-83.

[50]Ibid.; Dulles, Yesterday in Mexico, 504.

without limitation, prohibited the coinage of new silver pesos, and expanded the rediscount functions of the Bank of Mexico. The bank was to function as a central bank of rediscount. As an indication of the importance attached to this new monetary policy, Calles was named president of the Bank of Mexico.[51]

The Plan Calles was deflationary and resulted in a scarcity of pesos. Calles, who remained the real source of power in Mexico, was embarrassed and annoyed by the failure of the plan that bore his name. Former Finance Minister Pani had been criticizing the monetary policy from the outset. The accuracy of his predictions so impressed Calles that he instructed Ortiz Rubio to replace Montes de Oca with Pani. This was done on January 20, 1932.

Meanwhile the Lamont-Montes de Oca agreement was dying a slow but steady death. No silver deposits under the supplementary agreement of January 1931 were made that year. Mexico's budgetary deficit had reached 31 million pesos by year end. On December 22, 1931, an interim agreement was concluded between the Committee and the Mexican government which recognized Mexico's fiscal plight and therefore suspend the Lamont-Montes de Oca accord and the supplementary agreement. It also provided for a return of the $5 million then on deposit with the Committee. Should Mexico become able

---

[51] Ibid., 505-506.

to redeposit that sum on or before July 1, 1933, the 1930 agreement would again go into effect, with the first annuity to be paid in 1934.[52]

A month later, on January 27, 1932, the Mexican Congress rejected the Lamont-Montes de Oca agreement and the supplementary accord, but it approved the interim agreement of December 1931. In view of the above developments the International Committee published an audited statement of its receipts on behalf of the bondholders covering the period from its formation until February 1, 1932. The statement indicated that receipts over the years had totalled approximately $44.9 million, of which almost $37.9 million had been distributed to the bondholders. The Committee revealed its intention to distribute the balance, some $6.9 million, as soon as the courts resolved conflicting legal claims to the funds.[53]

The new Finance Minister Pani made dramatic efforts to turn the tide of the depression in Mexico. On March 9, 1932, a new monetary reform law was enacted which replaced the disastrous Plan Calles. It provided for unlimited coinage

---

[52] Wynne, State Insolvency, 84-85.

[53] Ibid., 85 fn. For State Department correspondence regarding the court cases see Telles to Stimson, April 16, 1931; Stimson to Franklin D. Roosevelt, April 27, 1931; Stimson to Tellez, April 27, 1931; Tellez to Stimson, June 26, 1931, all in FRUS 1931, II, 729-733.

of silver pesos containing less silver than the marked
value. The profit was to be added to the legal reserves
of the Bank of Mexico. This would enable the bank to issue
more paper money, freely convertible into silver.[54] The
result of the Pani program was to depreciate the peso in
relations to the dollar but to increase the amount of paper currency in circulation from 4 million pesos on March
9, 1932, to 20 million pesos on June 23, 1932.[55]

Despite these efforts, Mexico's income for the first
eight months of 1932 amounted to only 227.7 million pesos.
This was approximately 4 million pesos less than its expenditures for the same period. This deficit included upaid
obligations carried over from 1931 and previous years.[56]

By August 1932 Ortiz Rubio was serving his last days
as president. He had scrupulously bowed to the wishes of
Calles throughout his presidency. All important posts were
filled with individuals Calles had designated. Cabinet members were frequently dismissed because Calles was displeased
with them. Few Mexican officials even bothered to pretend

---

[54] Alberto J. Pani, Mi contribución al nuevo régimen, 1910-1933 (Mexico City, 1936), 332-337, 344.

[55] Statement by Pani, June 28, 1932, quoted in Report of the Acting Military Attaché, Captain Robert E. Cummings, July 12, 1932, Records of the Office of the Chief of Naval Operations, Office of Naval Intelligence, National Archives, Record Group 38.

[56] Presidential Message, September 1, 1932, in Report of the Acting Military Attaché, September 5, 1932, ibid.

that Ortiz Rubio was the chief executive. The president himself frequently acknowledged that he owed his position solely to Calles.

In late August 1932 Ortiz Rubio angered Calles by making an unpopular choice as director of Mexico's largest hospital. The post was relatively insignificant and Ortiz Rubio acted without consulting Calles. For reasons that are not clear, Calles took offense at this show of independence and ordered his followers to refuse to accept any posts offered them by Ortiz Rubio. Thus the president found it impossible to fill vacant offices with "true revolutionaries" in the Calles mold. Disturbed by these developments and in ill-health, Ortiz Rubio offered his resignation. After considerable backstage maneuvering Albelardo Rodrígues, another Calles' puppet, was named to fill out the remainder of the term. He was sworn in as interim president on September 4, 1932.[57]

Simultaneously, in the United States, the depression was bringing an end to the long political career of Herbert Hoover. Two months after Ortiz Rubio's resignation, the third Democratic president in seventy-two years, Franklin D. Roosevelt, was elected. In his inaugural speech, on March 4, 1933, Roosevelt, borrowing the term "good neighbor" from Hoover, declared that "In the field of world policy I would

---

[57]Dulles, <u>Yesterday in Mexico</u>, 533-543.

dedicate this Nation to the policy of the good neighbor." To implement the policy in Mexico, Roosevelt appointed as ambassador his good friend and World War I boss, Josephus Daniels.

During the 1920's changes in the Mexican executive office, and to a lesser extent in the White House, had caused great anxiety among the International Committee of Bankers. The two most recent changes that occurred within a few months of each other appeared to make no difference to the Committee. The persistent worldwide depression rendered its goals unattainable in the near future. This is not to say that Lamont ceased to pursue the elusive definitive accord. Quite to the contrary, Lamont contacted the new ambassador prior to his departure for Mexico City in the hopes that he would be more cooperative with the Committee than Morrow and Clark had been. Daniels was totally unsympathetic and refused to see Lamont. Although Daniels was primarily motivated by an almost irrational distrust of all bankers, he believed that other American claims against Mexico should have priority over those of the bondholders, whom he believed were mainly speculators in pursuit of windfall profits rather than the original investors.[58]

The interim agreement between the Mexican government

---

[58] E. David Cronon, *Josephus Daniels in Mexico* (Madison, 1960), 118-119.

and the Committee had set July 1, 1933, as the terminal date for redeposit of funds under terms of the Lamont-Montes de Oca accord. When no funds were deposited the interim agreement lapsed. In his first annual message to Congress, on September 1, 1933, President Rodrígues claimed that his administration had deliberately allowed the agreement to expire, since its terms were burdensome and Mexico had no intention, in view of its fiscal debility, to allow large sums to be sent out of the nation annually.[59]

As early as April 1933, the Mexican government apparently had determined that it could not or would not prevent the interim agreement from lapsing. It began to press the Committee to return those funds (approximately $6.9 million) that it held on behalf of the bondholders it represented. The Mexicans claimed that the return of these funds would benefit the bondholders since it would assist the government in its efforts to stabilize exchange rates. The Committee refused unless the return of funds was to be an initial step in a program aimed at the resumption of payments under terms of the Lamont-Montes de Oca agreement. Mexico refused to commit itself to this.[60]

Although negotiations between the Committee and the Mexican government continued throughout 1933 and into 1934, no new understanding was possible. The growing influence

---

[59] Wynne, State Insolvency, 85-86.

[60] Munroe to Morgan, Grenfell & Company, June 21, 1933, Box 192, Lamont Papers.

of a new generation of Marxist politicians, the refusal of Ambassador Daniels to cooperate,[61] and most importantly the impact of the depression on Mexico made a new agreement unthinkable. On May 21, 1934, the Mexican government officially broke off relations with the International Committee. Sporadic attempts to reopen negotiations later in the decade failed. Mexican claims to the funds held by the Committee were disallowed by American courts in 1942, 1944 and 1945. It was not until 1948 that the Committee finally distributed the monies it held.[62]

---

[61] In late 1933 the State Department unofficially sponsored the formation of a Foreign Bondholders Protective Council. The group's aim was to attempt to bring about a general settlement of Latin American indebtedness to American citizens. Daniels opposed the Council on grounds that it smacked of "dollar diplomacy." Cronon, Josephus Daniels, 117-118.

[62] Wynne, State Insolvency, 103-104 fn.

CONCLUSION

Between 1919 and 1924 the Department of State and the International Committee of Bankers on Mexico cooperated in an effort to reduce tensions between the United States and Mexico and to protect the interests of foreign holders of Mexican securities. The State Department and the International Committee worked together because they shared common interests and goals. The Committee hoped that a normalization of relations would facilitate Mexico's return to fiscal responsibility including the protection of foreign investments. The State Department believed that Mexico's financial reconstruction would contribute to the maintenance of good relations between the two countries.

At a time when influential American oil interests were aggressively lobbying for armed intervention to protect their property rights, the State Department and the International Committee called for and employed moderation in their dealings with Mexico. They rejected the threat of force but maintained the traditional American reverence for private property.

The close cooperation between the Department and the Committee continued until the appointment of James Rockwell Sheffield as Ambassador to Mexico. Sheffield took a stance closely akin to that of the oil interests. He repeatedly advocated a "hard line" and made clear his preference for armed intervention.

Sheffield's appointment was particularly unfortunate in that he antagonized the Mexicans at a time when the goals of American financial diplomacy seemed achievable (as evidenced by the Bucareli and Lamont-de la Huerta agreements). Frank B. Kellogg, the new Secretary of State, and Thomas W. Lamont, Chairman of the International Committee, found it impossible to work with Sheffield. They circumvented the ambassador and dealt with the Mexican leaders directly. This was not conducive to a united effort.

In September 1925 Kellogg turned over Mexican policy decisions to Robert E. Olds, the new assistant secretary. Olds slowly developed a new, more "enlightened" approach to Mexican-American relations. The fundamental tenet of the Olds policy was that the United States must find some way of "getting along" with its southern neighbor. Protection of property rights and investments was important but should not be allowed to jeopardize good relations with Mexico. Sheffield opposed this policy vehemently.

In 1927 Dwight W. Morrow replaced Sheffield as ambassador and immediately began implementing the "softer" policy emanating from the State Department. He enjoyed great initial success in alleviating several sources of friction between the two nations. Morrow's attempts to unwind Mexico's complex financial problems, however, brought him into conflict with Lamont.

Until 1927 Lamont had had the approval of the State Department to pursue an agreement with Mexico on behalf of the bondholders he represented. Twice he succeeded in concluding accords--the Lamont-de la Huerta and Lamont-Pani agreements--only to have unexpected events in Mexico nullify his efforts. In 1928 Morrow and the Department came to believe that Mexico was an insolvent nation and that separate agreements with individual groups of creditors were contrary to Mexico's interests and endangered Mexican-American relations. They suggested that Mexico's debts could only be honored through some pro rata settlement with all classes of creditors in a general plan under bankruptcy-like conditions.

Lamont disagreed with these contentions but Morrow and the Department were adamant. Lamont, therefore, ceased to cooperate with the State Department and singlemindedly pursued a separate accord with Mexico covering the holdings of bondholders represented by his committee.

Under Kellogg and Henry L. Stimson, his successor, the State Department recognized the hypersensitivity of the Mexican revolutionary generation to anything which even remotely resembled "big stick" diplomacy. Policymakers were aware that hemispherical harmony required that the United States abandon the old, high-handed manner of dealing with its neighbors and become a "good neighbor." In order to accomplish this it was necessary that the long-standing intimate and sometimes unholy relationship between private American business and banking interests and the State Department be terminated. Although this did not come about over night, it is evident that from 1925 the State Department began to pursue a policy with regard to Mexico (and eventually all of Latin America) that was more progressive than many private interests desired. Franklin Roosevelt is frequently given credit for this "good neighbor" policy but it had its genesis in the Coolidge-Kellogg administration and was advanced further under Hoover and Stimson.

BIBLIOGRAPHY

Primary Sources

Manuscripts, Typescripts, and Private Papers

House, Edward M. Papers, Yale University Library, New Haven, Connecticut.

Lamont, Thomas W. Papers, Baker Library, Harvard Graduate School of Business Administration, Boston, Massachusetts.

McBride, Captain Lewis B. Papers. In possession of Mrs. Lewis B. McBride, Washington, D.C.

Morrow, Dwight W. Papers, Amherst College Library, Amherst, Massachusetts.

Polk, Frank L. Papers, Yale University Library, New Haven, Connecticut.

U.S. Department of Navy. Reports of the Naval Attaché, Records of the Office of the Chief of Naval Operations, Office of Naval Intelligence, National Archives, Record Group 38.

Memoirs, Diaries, and Reminiscences

Grew, Joseph C. (Walter Johnson, ed.) Turbulent Era: A Diplomatic Record of Forty Years, 1904-1945 (2 vols., Boston, 1952).

Guzman, Martin Luis. (trans. V.H. Taylor) Memoirs of Pancho Villa (Austin, 1965).

Pani, Alberto J. Mi contribución al nuevo régimen, 1910-1933 (Mexico City, 1936).

Portes Gil, Emilio. Quince años de política mexicana (2nd ed., Mexico City, 1941).

Rublee, George. "The Reminiscences of George Rublee" (Oral History Research Office, Columbia University, New York, 1951).

Stimson, Henry L. and McGeorge Bundy. On Active Service in Peace and War (New York, 1947).

Williams, James T. "The Reminiscences of James T. Williams" (2 vols., Oral History Research Office, Columbia University, New York, 1957).

Wilson, Henry Lane. Diplomatic Episodes in Mexico, Belgium and Chile (Garden City, N.Y., 1927).

Wilson, Hugh. Diplomat Between Wars (New York, 1941).

Government Documents

Mexico. Secretaría de Hacienda y Crédito Público. La controversia Pani-De la Huerta: Documentos para la Historia de la última Asonda Militar (Mexico City, 1924).

Mexico. Secretaría de Hacienda y Crédito Público. La deuda exterior de México (Mexico City, 1926).

Mexico. Secretaría de Hacienda y Crédito Público. Memoria de la Secretaría de Hacienda y Crédito Público correspondiente a los años fiscales de 1923, 1924, 1925 (Mexico City, 1926).

Mexico. Secretaría de Relaciones Exteriores. La cuestión internacional mexicano-americana durante el gobierno del Gral. Don Alvaro Obregón (3rd ed., Mexico City, 1949).

United States. Department of State. Proceedings of the United States-Mexican Commission Convened at Mexico City, May 14, 1923 (Washington, D.C., 1925).

United States. Department of State. Papers Relating to the Foreign Relations of the United States Vols. for 1867, 1877, 1878, 1919-1922, 1925, 1928-1931. (Washington, D.C., 1867-1956).

United States. Senate, Committee on Foreign Relations, 66th Cong., 2nd Sess., series 7665-7666. *Investigation of Mexican Affairs* (2 vols., Washington, D.C., 1920).

United States. Senate, 71st Cong., Special Sess., *Inaugural Address by President Herbert Hoover, March 4, 1929* (Washington, D.C., 1929).

United States. Senate, 71st Cong., 2nd Sess., *Memorandum on the Monroe Doctrine, Prepared by J. Reuben Clark, Undersecretary of State* (Washington, D.C., 1930).

Other Sources and Unpublished Works

Addresses Delivered During the Visit of Herbert Hoover, President-elect of the United States, to Central and South America, November-December 1928 (Washington, D.C., 1929).

Calles, Plutarco Elías. (Robert H. Murray, ed. and trans.) *Mexico Before the World: Public Documents and Addresses of Plutarco Elías Calles* (New York, 1927).

Clark, J. Reuben. "The Oil Settlement with Mexico," *Foreign Affairs*, VI (July 1928), 600-614.

McBride, Mrs. Lewis B. to author, August 17, 1974.

Report of the Council of the Corporation of Foreign Bondholders (London, 1886 and 1899).

Second Annual Report of the Council of the Corporation of Foreign Bondholders (London, 1874).

Sterrett, Joseph E. *The Fiscal and Economic Conditions of Mexico: Supplemental Report Dated November 15, 1928* (New York, 1928).

Stimson, Henry L. "Bases of American Foreign Policy During the Past Four Years," *Foreign Affairs*, XI (April 1933), 383-396.

Secondary Works

Alba, Victor. Horizon Concise History of Mexico (New York, 1973).

Baring, Evelyn. Modern Egypt (2 vols., New York, 1908-1909).

Bazant, Jan. La deuda exterior de México, 1823-1946 (Mexico City, 1968).

Bernstein, Marvin. The Mexican Mining Industry, 1890-1950: A Study of the Interaction of Politics, Economics, and Technology (Albany, 1966).

Callcott, Wilfred H. Liberalism in Mexico, 1857-1929 (Palo Alto, Cal., 1931).

Clendenen, Clarence C. Blood on the Border: The United States Army and the Mexican Irregulars (New York, 1969).

Cline, Howard F. The United States and Mexico (rev. ed., Cambridge, 1967).

Cockcroft, James. Intellectual Precursors of the Mexican Revolution, 1900-1913 (Austin, 1968).

Cronon, E. David. Josephus Daniels in Mexico (Madison, 1960).

Cumberland, Charles C. The Mexican Revolution: Genesis Under Madero (Austin, 1952).

Cumberland, Charles C. The Mexican Revolution: The Constitutionalist Years (Austin, 1972).

DeConde, Alexander. Herbert Hoover's Latin American Policy (Stanford, 1951).

Dulles, Foster Rhea. America's Rise to World Power (New York, 1954).

Dulles, John W.F. Yesterday in Mexico: A Chronicle of the Revolution, 1919-1936 (Austin, 1961).

Dunn, Frederick S. The Diplomatic Protection of Americans in Mexico (New York, 1933).

Ellis, L. Ethan. Frank B. Kellogg and American Foreign Relations, 1925-1929 (New Brunswick, N.J., 1961).

Haley, P. Edward. Revolution and Intervention: The Diplomacy of Taft and Wilson with Mexico, 1910-1917 (Cambridge, 1970).

Hill, Larry D. Emissaries to a Revolution: Woodrow Wilson's Executive Agents in Mexico (Baton Rouge, 1973).

Kemmerer, Edwin W. Inflation and Revolution: Mexico's Experience of 1912-1917 (Princeton, 1940).

Link, Arthur S. Wilson the Diplomatist (Chicago, 1957).

Link, Arthur S. Woodrow Wilson and the Progressive Era (New York, 1954).

MacCorkle, Stuart A. The American Policy of Recognition Toward Mexico (Baltimore, 1933).

Morison, Elting E. Turmoil and Tradition: A Study of the Life and Times of Henry L. Stimson (New York, 1960).

Munro, Dana. The United States and the Caribbean Republics, 1921-1933 (Princeton, 1974).

Murray, Robert K. The Harding Era (Minneapolis, 1969).

Nicolson, Harold. Dwight Morrow (New York, 1935).

Pani, Alberto J. Las Conferencias de Bucareli (Mexico City, 1953).

Powell, Fred W. The Railways of Mexico (Boston, 1921).

Quirk, Robert E. An Affair of Honor: Woodrow Wilson and the Occupation of Veracruz (Lexington, 1962).

Rice, Elizabeth Ann. The Diplomatic Relations between the United States and Mexico as Affected by the Struggle for Religious Liberty in Mexico: 1925-1929 (Washington, D.C., 1959).

Rippy, J. Fred, José Vasconcelos and Guy Stevens. American Policies Abroad: Mexico (Chicago, 1928).

Roaix, Pastor. Genesis de los articulos 27 y 123 de la Constitución Politica de 1917 (Mexico City, 1959).

Ross, Stanley R. Francisco I. Madero, Apostle of Mexican Democracy (New York, 1955).

Scholes, Walter V. *Mexican Politics during the Juárez Regime, 1855-1872* (Columbia, Mo., 1957).

Scott, James B. *The Hague Convention and Declarations of 1899 and 1907* (New York, 1915).

Simpson, Eyler N. *The Ejido: Mexico's Way Out* (Chapel Hill, N.C., 1937).

Smith, Daniel M. *Aftermath of War: Bainbridge Colby and Wilsonian Diplomacy, 1920-1921* (Philadelphia, 1970).

Smith, Robert F. *The United States and Revolutionary Nationalism in Mexico, 1916-1932* (Chicago, 1972).

Stephenson, George M. *John Lind of Minnesota* (Minneapolis, 1935).

Sweetman, Jack. *The Landing at Veracruz: 1914* (Annapolis, 1968).

Tannenbaum, Frank. *Mexico: The Struggle for Peace and Bread* (New York, 1950).

Tulchin, Joseph S. *The Aftermath of War: World War I and United States Policy Toward Latin America* (New York, 1971).

Turlington, Edgar. *Mexico and Her Foreign Creditors* (New York, 1930).

Womack, Jr., John. *Zapata and the Mexican Revolution* (New York, 1969).

Wynne, William H. *State Insolvency and Foreign Bondholders: Selected Case Histories of Governmental Foreign Bond Defaults and Debt Readjustments* (New Haven, 1951).

Zea, Leopoldo. *El positivismo en Mexico* (Mexico City, 1953).

Periodical Articles

Bullington, John P. "Problems of International Law in the Mexican Constituion of 1917," *American Journal of International Law*, XXI (October 1927), 685-705.

Cumberland, Charles C. "The Jenkins Case and Mexican-American Relations," *Hispanic American Historical Review*, XXXI (November 1951), 586-607.

Ellis, L. Ethan. "Dwight Morrow and the Church-State Controversy in Mexico," *Hispanic American Historical Review*, XXXVIII (November 1958), 482-505.

Glaser, David. "1919: William Jenkins, Robert Lansing, and the Mexican Interlude," *Southwestern Historical Quarterly*, LXXIV (January 1971), 337-356.

Kane, N. Stephen. "Bankers and Diplomats: The Diplomacy of the Dollar in Mexico, 1921-1924," *Business History Review*, LXVII (Autumn 1973), 335-352.

Machado, Manuel A. and James T. Judge. "Tempest in a Teapot? The Mexican-United States Intervention Crisis of 1919," *Southwestern Historical Quarterly*, LXXIV (July 1970), 1-23.

Ross, Stanley R. "Dwight Morrow and the Mexican Revolution," *Hispanic American Historical Review*, XXXVIII (November 1958), 506-528.

Trow, Clifford W. "Woodrow Wilson and the Mexican Interventionist Movement of 1919," *Journal of American History*, LVIII (June 1971), 46-72.

Titles in the Series

1. Donald C. Baldridge, *Mexican Petroleum and United States-Mexican Relations, 1919-1923*
2. Robert W. Barrie, *Congress and the Executive: The Making of the United States Foreign Trade Policy, 1789-1968*
3. Kenneth L. Bauge, *Voluntary Export Restriction as a Foreign Commercial Policy with Special Reference to Japanese Cotton Textiles, 1930-1962*
4. George D. Beelen, *Harding and Mexico: Diplomacy by Economic Persuasion, 1920-1923*
5. Stephen D. Bodayla, *Financial Diplomacy: The United States and Mexico, 1919-1933*
6. Jonathan E. Boe, *American Business: The Response to the Soviet Union, 1933-1947*
7. Joseph R. Cammarosano, *The Contributions of John Maynard Keynes to Foreign Trade Theory and Policy, 1909-1946*
8. Charles Carreras, *United States Economic Penetration of Venezuela and its Effects on Diplomacy, 1895-1906*
9. Rex J. Casillas, *Oil and Diplomacy, The Evolution of America Foreign Policy in Saudi Arabia, 1933-1945*
10. Julia Fukuda Cosgrove, *United States Foreign Economic Policy Toward China, 1943-1946: From the End of Extraterritoriality to the Sino-American Commercial Treaty of 1946*
11. Brian P. Damiani, *Advocates of Empire: William McKinley, the Senate and American Expansion, 1898-1899*
12. Clarence B. Davis, *Partners and Rivals: Britain's Imperial Diplomacy Concerning the United States and Japan in China, 1915-1922*

13. Leonard F. Giesecke, *History of American Economic Policy in the Philippines During the Colonial Period, 1900-1935*

14. Kenneth A. Gold, *United States Foreign Economic Policy-Making: An Analysis of the Use of Food Resources, 1972-1980*

15. Thomas J. Heston, *Sweet Subsidy: The Economic and Diplomatic Effects of the U. S. Sugar Acts, 1934-1974*

16. Michael W. Hodin, *A National Policy for Organized Free Trade: The Case of U. S. Foreign Trade Policy for Steel, 1976-1978*

17. William F. Kolarik, Jr., *A Model for the Study of International Trade Politics: The United States Business Community and Soviet-American Relations, 1975-1976*

18. Robert Stanley Mayer, *The Influence of Frank A. Vanderlip and the National City Bank on American Commerce and Foreign Policy, 1910-1920*

19. William George Pullen, *World War Debts and United States Foreign Policy, 1919-1929*

20. Emily S. Rosenberg, *World War I and the Growth of United States Predominance in Latin America*

21. Benjamin M. Rowland, *Commercial Conflict and Foreign Policy: A Study in Anglo-American Relations, 1932-1938*

22. William F. Sanford, Jr., *The American Business Community and the European Recovery Program, 1947-1952*

23. Dale N. Shook, *William G. McAdoo and the Development of National Economic Policy, 1913-1918*

24. Joseph Short, *American Business and Foreign Policy: Cases in Coffee and Cocoa Trade Regulation, 1961-1974*

Augsburg College
George Sverdrup Library
Minneapolis, MN 55454